Entertaining Economically

MARGUERITE PATTEN

TREASURE PRESS

WEIGHTS AND MEASURES

All measurements in this book are based on Imperial weights and measures.

When a cup measurement is used, this refers to a cup of 8 fl. oz. capacity.

1 Imperial pint = 20 fl. oz.

Level spoon measurements are used in all the recipes.

Metric measures: for easy reference

1 kilogramme (1000 grammes) = 2.2 lb

$\frac{1}{2}$ kilogramme (500 grammes) = 1 lb (working equivalent)

1 litre = $1\frac{3}{4}$ pints (working equivalent)

$\frac{1}{2}$ litre = 1 pint (working equivalent)

Previous page: MELON BALLS WITH LEMON SAUCE

Acknowledgments

The publishers would like to thank the following organizations for their kind permission to reproduce the pictures in this book: Argentine Beef Bureau, *page* 45; Cadbury Schweppes Food Advisory Service, Bournville, Birmingham., *page* 73; John Lee, pages 1, 13, 17, 21, 36, 41, 49, 57, 81, 105, 113; John West Foods Limited, *page* 25; RHM Foods Limited, *page* 65; Syndication International, pages 5, 9, 28, 29, 33, 37, 53, 61, 69, 77, 85, 89, 93, 97, 101, 109, 121.

First published by Octopus Books Limited
This edition published by Treasure Press
59 Grosvenor Street
London W1

© 1973 Octopus Books Limited

ISBN 0 907407 18 8

Printed in Hong Kong

Contents

Weights and Measures   2

Introduction   4

Hors d'oeuvre   6

Choosing soups 22

Choosing fish dishes 30

Choosing meat dishes 40

Choosing vegetable dishes 68

Choosing salads 76

Choosing desserts 78

Choosing savouries 110

Choosing wines 112

Parties 115

Tea and Coffee parties 118

Picnics and Barbecues 122

Entertaining children 125

Introduction

Do not imagine that expensive foods and elaborate dishes are essential if you wish to entertain successfully. With a little imagination and know-how, the cheaper foods can provide most delicious and interesting menus. This book suggests a number of recipes from which to choose when entertaining your friends.

If you have little time for cooking then look at the savoury section and the dips etc., see pages 14 and 110, and ask your friends to come for a drink and a snack.

You may prefer to invite them to tea or coffee and provide one or two interesting cakes or gâteaux. These can be made before-hand, so you have no last-minute scramble.

If you enjoy cooking then undoubtedly you would rather have a leisurely luncheon or dinner party and there are a number of dishes that contribute to a well-balanced meal.

Whatever the occasion there are certain rules for successful entertaining:

Firstly – a relaxed hostess and host – so plan well ahead and choose dishes that cannot spoil if they are kept waiting. You will find hints on some pages for early preparation of the food and suggestions for keeping them hot without spoiling.

Secondly – choose dishes that look colourful and attractive, as well as tasting delicious, and make sure your menu is varied in flavour, colour and texture.

PATE DE GRILLOTIN

Hors D'Oeuvre

There are many economical ingredients from which to select the first course of the meal, or more expensive ingredients may be blended with these cheaper foods, for example:

When avocado pears are expensive: Slice peeled and stoned avocado pears, toss carefully in oil, vinegar and seasoning and arrange on a bed of lettuce with an equal amount of grapefruit segments. Also see suggestions on pages 14 and 18.

If melons are costly: Dice the fruit, blend with grapefruit segments and orange slices.

If shell fish costs more than you wish to spend make a **mixed fish cocktail:** Cook white fish, blend with mayonnaise, flavour with tomato purée and anchovy essence. Put shredded lettuce in glasses, place fish mixture on lettuce, and top with shell fish and lemon.

To eke out smoked salmon: Serve portions of lightly scrambled egg, topped with chopped chives, with the fish. Make smoked salmon into a pâté (see page 16), which could be made with scraps – often obtainable from fishmongers.

Fresh vegetables make an ideal first course. The most suitable are artichokes, asparagus and courgettes.
Both asparagus and artichokes are equally good served hot with melted butter or cold with a vinaigrette dressing and courgettes can be turned into a hot or cold dish (see page 75). Although ratatouille makes an excellent vegetable dish to serve with the main course it is equally good as an hors d'oeuvre – here again you can choose whether to serve it hot or cold.

INSTEAD OF HORS D'OEUVRE

It may be more simple for you to omit an hors d'oeuvre and to serve canapés and various savoury dishes with pre-dinner drinks. The recipes that follow are equally suitable for this purpose and for cocktail or buffet parties.

Canapés

It is important to choose a good base for the savoury ingredients. Toast will soften when left standing for any length of time. I prefer crisply fried and well drained pieces of bread or small pieces of buttered white, brown, rye or crispbread. If you like a really crisp biscuit base remember these will soften if you spread them with a soft pâté, so keep these for firm cheese mixtures.

Some economical toppings for canapés:

a) Pâté, topped with cocktail onions or sliced gherkins or pieces of red pepper.

b) Shell fish, blended with scrambled egg or thick mayonnaise.

c) Small rounds of ham or salami, decorated with cream cheese.

d) Cheese spreads – made by blending grated cheese or soft cream cheese with mayonnaise and any other flavourings required, curry powder, Tabasco sauce, etc.

e) Smoked salmon or other smoked fish, topped with asparagus tips or scrambled egg.

Cheese Biscuits, made with the cheese pastry on page 19, form an ideal base for canapés, or cut the pastry into fingers for cheese straws. Although cheese straws are served at the end of the meal with cheese, or are often an accompaniment to soup, particularly turtle soup, they are one of the easiest and most popular cocktail savouries.

Fashions change in the kind of food offered, and dips are becoming more popular. They are quick to make, can be as luxurious or economical as you wish. You will find some suggestions on pages 14 and 15.

Frosted Tomato Cocktail

Although this cocktail can be served to everyone at the beginning of a meal, without the choice of an alternative, I occasionally have made it part of a mixed hors d'oeuvre, for it balances the rather rich flavour of foods in mayonnaise. In this case scoop out balls of the frosted mixture and serve on a bed of lettuce.

2 lb. ripe tomatoes
4 tablespoons water
seasoning
good pinch sugar

little lemon juice
Worcestershire sauce to taste
Garnish:
lettuce or mint

Chop the tomatoes. Put into a saucepan with the water, seasoning and sugar. Heat for a few minutes only so you can extract the juice. Rub through a sieve or emulsify. Add lemon juice, Worcestershire sauce and any extra seasoning or flavouring required – celery salt, cayenne pepper and a few drops chilli sauce can be added. Put into the freezing tray and freeze lightly.
Either spoon or scoop on to lettuce leaves and make part of a mixed hors d'oeuvre, or chop lightly and spoon into chilled glasses and top with mint leaves.
Serves 4–6, or 8–12 if part of a mixed hors d'oeuvre.

Variation:
Frosted Melon Cocktail: The red fleshed water melon is ideal. Halve the melon, remove the seeds and scoop out the flesh. Mix with lemon juice, a little sugar, then taste. You may like to add seasoning to make it more piquant in flavour and/or a few drops chilli or Worcestershire sauce. Freeze and serve as the tomato cocktail above.

To prepare in advance:
This must be prepared early, since it needs time to frost adequately. It can be stored in a freezer or freezing compartment for some time. Do not serve it too cold though.

Economy hint:
When tomatoes are expensive use canned or bottled tomato juice and omit the water.

Melon Balls with Lemon Sauce

1 melon, see below
2 lemons
little water
2 tablespoons sugar

Garnish:
sprigs of mint
twists of lemon

Buy a ripe Honeydew, Charentais or Cantaloupe melon, or a rather large Ogen melon. Halve the melon, and remove the seeds. Take a vegetable scoop and make balls of the flesh. Chill these. The rather untidy pieces of melon at the bottom of the fruit can be used for the sauce.

Grate enough rind from the lemons to give about 2 teaspoons. Squeeze the juice, measure and add enough water to give $\frac{1}{4}$ pint ($\frac{2}{3}$ cup). Simmer the rind with the liquid and sugar for about 5 minutes. Pour over the odd pieces of melon, then sieve or emulsify in the liquidizer. Taste and add more sugar if wished. This is not really necessary, for the sauce should be both thick and fairly sharp. Spoon into the bottom of 4–6 glasses and top with the melon balls. Garnish with mint and lemon.

Serves 4–6.

Variations:
Sprinkle the balls of melon with a little Crème de Menthe. Freeze canned pineapple juice until lightly frozen; do not allow it to become too hard. Put at the bottom of glasses and top with diced melon or melon balls.

To prepare in advance:
Cut the melon balls and prepare the syrup, but do not blend until 1–2 hours before the meal so the melon does not become over-soft.

New ways to serve:
Toss the melon balls in the syrup and serve as a dessert rather than an hors d'oeuvre. It is delicious with ice cream or with cream.

Pâté De Grillotin (French Pork Pâté)

1 lb. pig's liver
8 oz. lean pork meat
8 oz. fat belly of pork
1–2 cloves garlic
1 shallot or small onion
2 oz. ($\frac{1}{4}$ cup) lard or butter
1 oz. ($\frac{1}{4}$ cup) flour

$\frac{1}{4}$ pint ($\frac{2}{3}$ cup) brown stock
1–2 teaspoons freshly chopped
    herbs
seasoning
little grated nutmeg
2–3 sage leaves
about 1 lb. fairly fat rashers bacon

Chop the liver, pork and belly of pork separately. If preferred put through a coarse mincer. Crush the garlic, chop the shallot or onion. Toss for a few minutes in the lard or butter, stir in the flour and blend the stock gradually into the mixture. Bring to the boil and thicken. Add the herbs, seasoning and nutmeg. Put in all the meat. If you wish the meat in the pâté to be clearly defined stir very little.
Put a few sage leaves at the bottom of a tin or oven-proof dish, then line the bottom and sides with the bacon. Spoon in the pâté. Cover with greased foil or paper. Stand in a container of water and bake in a slow to very moderate oven, 300–325°F, Mark 2–3 for about $1\frac{1}{4}$ hours. Allow to cool in the tin and place a small weight on top; this makes it easier to slice the pâté. Serve with hot toast and butter.
Serves 8–10.

Variations:
For a more luxurious pâté add 1–2 tablespoons brandy and a few skinned pistachio nuts.
For a creamier, smoother pâté use half pork and half calf's liver and thin cream or milk instead of stock. Put the meat through a mincer two or three times.

Economy hints:
This is a particularly economical pâté, but if served with a simple mixed salad, including sliced hard boiled eggs, it will serve about 12–14 people.

11

Artichokes Vinaigrette

artichokes
salt

oil and vinegar dressing,
see page 76

Wash the artichokes in cold salted water. Cut away any stalk and pull off any rather tough outer leaves. You can cut the tops of the leaves in a straight line with scissors, if wished. Cook the whole artichokes in boiling salted water until tender. The time varies – small very young artichokes take about 25 minutes, very large ones take about 40 minutes. Test to see if you can pull away a leaf.
To serve hot: Drain and serve with melted butter.
To serve cold: Make an oil and vinegar dressing, see page 76, season well and either spoon into the centre of each artichoke or serve separately.

Note:
If you wish to serve the dressing in the centre of the cold artichoke, then pull out the centre part of the vegetable. It is easier to do this when just warm; then allow it to cool.

Variation:
Serve cooked or canned asparagus as artichokes above.

Asparagus Parmesan

cooked or canned asparagus
little butter

grated Parmesan cheese

Drain the asparagus and heat gently in a little butter. Arrange carefully in a flame-proof dish, and top with a thick coating of Parmesan cheese. Brown for a few minutes under a hot grill.

Variation:
Asparagus Polanaise: Fry coarse breadcrumbs in hot butter, mix with chopped hard boiled eggs and chopped parsley and/or chopped chives and put over the asparagus just before serving.

Avocado Cream Dip

2 avocado pears
2 tablespoons lemon juice
3 tablespoons mayonnaise
1 very small onion or 2–3 spring
   onions or scallions
2 tablespoons soured cream

2 tablespoons thick cream
seasoning
Garnish:
shelled prawns or salted peanuts

Halve the avocado pears, remove the stones. Spoon out the
pulp into a basin; be careful not to break the skins, as these
will be used for holding the filling. Add the lemon juice at
once, so the pulp does not have an opportunity to discolour.
Mash thoroughly, then blend in all the other ingredients; the
onion, spring onions or scallions should be chopped very
finely. Return the mixture to the 4 halved shells and top with
prawns or nuts.
Serves 4, or 8–12 if part of a mixed hors d'oeuvre.

Variations:
Add 2–3 oz. (about $\frac{1}{2}$ cup) chopped prawns to the mixture.
Use cream cheese instead of thick cream and add finely
chopped nuts to the mixture.
Omit the avocado pear pulp, use 12 oz. ($1\frac{1}{2}$ cups) cottage or
cream cheese.
Flavour the basic recipe with curry powder.

To prepare in advance:
The tartlet cases on page 18 can be baked beforehand and
stored in an airtight tin, away from other foods. If they have
become slightly soft, warm in the oven. Make the avocado
pear filling earlier in the day, being generous with the lemon
juice so the mixture does not discolour. Put the filling into the
tartlet cases at the last minute.
The dip on this page can be made beforehand and covered, to
keep the colour and moist texture.
Always add the lemon juice to the avocado pears immediately
they are peeled and mashed.

Kipper and Grapefruit Dip

2 rashers lean bacon
1 small onion
2 fairly large grapefruit
12 oz. (1½ cups) cottage cheese
6 tablespoons thick cream

2 tablespoons chopped parsley
1 can kipper fillets
seasoning

Fry or grill the bacon until crisp, leave two larger pieces for garnish, then chop finely. Chop or grate the onion. Remove the tops from the grapefruit and scoop out all the pulp. Press this through a sieve to extract the juice. Mix the juice with the cottage cheese, the chopped bacon and onion and the cream. Blend thoroughly, then add the parsley and the well drained flaked kipper fillets. Keep two pieces of kipper for garnish. Season the mixture well, pile back into the grapefruit cases. Garnish with the pieces of bacon and kipper.
Serves 4, or 8–12 if part of a mixed hors d'oeuvre.

Melon and Pineapple Dip

1 Charentais or large Ogen melon
1 lb. (2 cups) cream cheese
5 oz. (⅔ cup) natural yogurt
1 tablespoon concentrated tomato
  purée

1 can pineapple pieces
2 tablespoons chopped parsley
seasoning

Cut the top off the melon, and scoop the flesh from the top. Remove the seeds then scoop out all the pulp; use a dessertspoon or a vegetable scoop. If using a scoop, save a few melon balls for garnish. Blend the cream cheese, yogurt and tomato purée until smooth. Stir in the melon pulp, well drained pineapple pieces and parsley. Mix thoroughly, add a little pineapple syrup from the can if the mixture is too stiff. Season well. Spoon back into the melon case and top with melon balls.
Serves 8, or 12–16 if part of a mixed hors d'oeuvre.

Taramasalata

8 oz. smoked cod's roe
2 oz. (up to $\frac{1}{4}$ cup) butter or
  2 tablespoons olive oil
1 lemon

pepper
1 clove garlic, optional
little chopped parsley

Remove all the skin from the roe. Blend the roe with the butter or oil, lemon juice to taste, pepper and a finely crushed clove of garlic. Put into a bowl and top with chopped parsley. Serve with hot toast, lemon and butter.
Serves up to 6.

Variations:
Blend the mixture above with about 2 tablespoons very fine soft crumbs.
Blend with 1 very smooth mashed potato; this makes a less rich pâté.
Halve the butter or oil and gradually whisk in 2–3 tablespoons warm water and the same amount of thin cream; flavour with chopped chives. This gives a mousse-like texture.
The liquidizer can be used to make this pâté; put the melted butter or oil, lemon juice and garlic into the goblet before the cod's roe.
Use freshly cooked or canned cod's roe and follow the recipe above, but flavour with a little anchovy essence and tomato purée to give both the colour and the salt flavour of smoked cod's roe.

More Fish Pâtés

Smoked Salmon Pâté:
Pound or emulsify pieces of smoked salmon and blend with melted butter, crushed garlic, cream, lemon juice and pepper. Mix well to give a creamy consistency.
Lightly cooked kippers, buckling or bloaters can be used in the same way as smoked cod's roe.

Avocado Tartlets

ingredients as cheese pastry,
  see page 19
1–2 egg whites
Filling:
2 large ripe avocado pears
2 tablespoons lemon juice

2 tablespoons thick mayonnaise
2–3 tablespoons whipped cream or
soft cream cheese
seasoning
Garnish:
watercress

Make the pastry as the basic recipe on page 19. Roll out
thinly and cut into rounds to line about 36 tiny cocktail
tartlet tins. Prick the base of the tarts with a fork, brush with
egg white to give a shine and bake as the Cheese Straws, see
page 19. Allow to cool. Do not fill until just before serving.
To make the filling: Halve the pears, remove the pulp, mash
with the lemon juice and mayonnaise, then blend with the
cream or cream cheese. Season well. Spoon into the tartlet
cases and top with watercress leaves. These small tartlet
cases may be cooked earlier and stored until ready to fill.
You can make a smaller amount of the avocado mixture, fill
some of the tartlet cases with this, then fill the rest with
scrambled eggs and chopped prawns, flaked cooked or
canned salmon and mayonnaise, or chopped ham blended with
cream cheese and mayonnaise.
Makes about 36.

Avocado and Bacon Rolls

Skin avocado pears, halve, take out the stones. Cut into thin
slices and dip in lemon juice. This is essential to prevent the
avocado becoming discoloured. Remove the rinds from rashers
of bacon, streaky bacon is best for this purpose. Halve the
rashers and wrap the bacon round the avocado pear. Secure
with wooden cocktail sticks. Cook in the oven or under the
grill until the bacon is crisp. Serve hot.

Cheese Pastry

This pastry is not only used for cheese straws and other cheese biscuits, but it can be used for tiny tartlet cases instead of short crust pastry.

8 oz. (2 cups) flour, preferably plain
good pinch salt
shake pepper
shake cayenne pepper
pinch dry mustard

4 oz. ($\frac{1}{2}$ cup) butter, margarine or cooking fat
3 oz. ($\frac{3}{8}$ cup) grated Parmesan cheese
2 egg yolks
water to mix

Sieve the dry ingredients together. Rub the butter, margarine or cooking fat into the flour. Add the cheese, then the egg yolks and sufficient water to make a rolling consistency. Roll out and use as the individual recipes.
You can make a batch of pastry and use it for several recipes.

Cheese Straws

Ingredients as Cheese Pastry recipe, see above, plus 1–2 egg whites. Roll out the pastry until about $\frac{1}{3}$ inch in thickness. Cut into fingers about $\frac{1}{3}$ inch in width and 3–4 inches in length. Lift on to well greased baking trays. Brush with egg white. Also cut out some rings of the pastry. Bake for 8–10 minutes towards the top of a hot oven, 425–450°F, Mark 6–7. Allow to cool on the tin, then lift off carefully and store in an airtight tin until ready to serve. When serving put some of the straws into the pastry rings.
Makes about 60 straws and 8–10 rings.

To prepare in advance:
Cheese straws should be kept in airtight tins away from other biscuits. Warm gently if desired to serve these hot.

19

Terrine of Chicken

1 roasting chicken, about $3\frac{1}{2}$ lb.
when trussed
the chicken giblets
about $\frac{3}{4}$ pint (about 2 cups) water
1 onion
bouquet garni
seasoning

6–8 oz. lean pork or veal, cut from
the top of the leg
approximately 12 oz. thin rashers
bacon
8 oz. (1 cup) pork sausagemeat
2 tablespoons chopped parsley

Cut all the meat from the bones of the chicken. Take great
care when removing the breast meat as this needs to be cut
later into neat slices. Put the chicken bones and the giblets
with the water, whole onion and herbs into a pan. Season well.
Put the lid on the pan and simmer for about 30 minutes.
Remove the lid and allow the liquid to boil rapidly to give
4 tablespoons really strong stock. Remove the liver.
Put the cooked chicken liver, all the dark meat (leave just
the breast), the pork or veal and 2 rashers of bacon through
a mincer, season well and blend with the sausagemeat and
2 tablespoons of the stock.
Slice the breast neatly, put on a dish, add the remaining stock
and the chopped parsley, season lightly.
Line the bottom of an oval or oblong oven-proof dish with
half the bacon rashers. Put a layer of the minced meat mixture
over the bacon, then add some of the sliced chicken breast.
Continue filling the dish like this, ending with minced meat.
Cover with bacon rashers. Put a well-fitting lid on the dish,
if available, and wrap foil round the outside, so no steam
escapes.
Stand the dish in a tin of cold water. Cook for $1\frac{1}{2}$ hours in the
centre of a very moderate oven, do not exceed 325°F, Mark 3.
Remove from the oven. Lift the lid carefully, as there is a
lot of steam trapped inside the dish. Put a light weight over
the terrine, so it is pressed into a neat shape as it cools. Turn
out when ready to serve. Serve cold with toast and butter or
with salad.
Serves 8–12 as an hors d'oeuvre or 4–6 as a main dish.

Choosing Soups

It is important to choose soups carefully for a special party. If the soup is too satisfying you spoil everyone's appetite for the rest of the meal.

If the soup is too strongly flavoured you cannot follow this with a very delicately flavoured main dish, you must choose something with an equally definite taste.

Beware of adding too much cream to a soup if you intend to serve a very creamy sauce with the main dish, or a dessert that is rich and creamy.

Consommé:

This is made by simmering shin of beef with vegetables to flavour, then straining it most carefully to produce a really clear liquid. Canned consommé is very good today and this can be given extra flavour with a little sherry and by adding interesting garnishes, i.e. dice or matchsticks of seasonal vegetables; tiny strips of pancake; pasta or rice.

Consommé can be served hot or lightly frozen or jellied – allow 2 teaspoons gelatine to each 1 pint ($2\frac{2}{3}$ cups) of the liquid. Soften the gelatine in a little cold consommé, heat the remainder of the soup and stir the gelatine into this. Allow to cool, set lightly then whisk and put into chilled soup cups. Serve with cheese straws, see page 19.

If the main course is meat or poultry, a vegetable or fish soup would be an ideal choice; but if you are serving fish then a chicken or meat soup would be a pleasing contrast.

Chowders are very satisfying so may precede a light salad.

Crab Bisque

1 medium-sized cooked crab
$\frac{3}{4}$ pint (2 cups) fish stock, see
  below, or water
1 lemon
seasoning
bouquet garni

1 onion
2 oz. ($\frac{1}{2}$ cup) mushrooms
2 oz. ($\frac{1}{4}$ cup) butter
$\frac{1}{2}$ pint ($1\frac{1}{3}$ cups) thin cream
2 egg yolks
2 tablespoons sherry

Remove all the meat from the crab, and put on one side. Put
the crab shell into a pan with the stock or water, the pared
lemon rind, a little lemon juice, seasoning and bouquet garni.
Cover the pan tightly and simmer for about 30 minutes.
Chop the onion, slice the mushrooms and toss in the hot
butter. Add the strained crab stock and crabmeat and heat
gently. Blend the cream with the egg yolks, add to the crab
mixture and heat, without boiling. Stir in the sherry, heat for
1–2 minutes and serve.
Serves 4–5.

To Make Fish Stock:
The crab shell, in the recipe above, produces a good
flavoured stock. Fish bones, skin and heads should be
simmered to give a really well flavoured fish stock to use in
fish soups and fish dishes.

Economy hint:
Use a mixture of white and shell fish in the recipe above.

To prepare in advance:
Make the stock; cook the vegetables in the recipe, but do not
cook the crabmeat in the soup for overcooked shell fish
becomes very tough and unpalatable.

New ways to serve:
This makes a delicious cold soup. Make the soup as above,
chill well and serve with wedges of lemon.

Salmon Chowder

1 pint (2⅔ cups) milk
medium-sized can sweet corn
medium-sized can salmon

1 oz. butter
seasoning
chopped parsley

Put the milk and sweet corn into a pan. Bring almost to the boil. Add the flaked salmon, butter, seasoning and parsley. Heat gently for a few minutes.
Serves 4.

Variations:

Use tuna, crabmeat, chopped prawns or flaked white fish in place of the salmon.
Omit the corn and add raw diced vegetables, such as potatoes, onions, peas, carrots, to the milk. Simmer steadily for about 15 minutes. Add a little extra milk or white stock, then the remaining ingredients.

Creamed Kidney Soup

1 onion
4 lambs' kidneys
2 oz. (¼ cups) butter or margarine
½ pint (1⅓ cups) stock

1 oz. (¼ cup) flour
¼ pint (⅔ cup) milk
seasoning
¼ pint (⅔ cup) thin cream
2 tablespoons sherry

Chop the onion and the kidneys very finely, and discard any gristle. Heat the butter or margarine and cook the onion and kidneys for a few minutes. Add the stock. Cover the pan and simmer gently for 15 minutes. Blend the flour with the milk, add to the kidney mixture, together with seasoning, and stir until thickened and smooth. Blend in the cream and sherry and heat without boiling for a few minutes.
Serves 4–5.

SALMON CHOWDER *(Photograph by John West Foods Ltd)*

Chicken Chowder

2 or 3 rashers bacon
1 onion
$\frac{3}{4}$ pint (2 cups) chicken stock
about 12 oz. ($1\frac{1}{2}$ cups) diced raw
   root vegetables
$\frac{1}{2}$ pint ($1\frac{1}{3}$ cups) milk
about 6 oz. (nearly 1 cup) diced
   cooked chicken

3–4 tablespoons sweet corn
seasoning
Garnish:
chopped parsley
paprika

Chop the bacon and the peeled onion. Fry the bacon for a few minutes. Add the onion then cook together until the bacon is crisp. Add the stock. Bring to the boil, put in the vegetables and cook until just tender. Add the milk, chicken, sweet corn and seasoning. Simmer for a few minutes then serve, topped with parsley and paprika.
Serves 4–6.

Variations:
Lobster Chowder: Use the recipe above, but add flaked lobster in place of the chicken. You can make the chowder with chicken stock or simmer the lobster shells to give a fish stock.
Ham Chowder: Use stock from boiling bacon or ham in place of chicken stock. Increase the amount of bacon slightly and reduce the amount of chicken.
Clam Chowder: Use fish stock in place of chicken stock and use about 8 oz. bacon. Add a medium-sized can clams instead of chicken.

Creamed Chicken Soup

Omit the sweet corn and the root vegetables in the Chicken Chowder recipe above. Sieve or emulsify the ingredients, including the cooked chicken. Top with cream before serving.

Crème Chambertin

2 medium-sized onions
2 medium-sized potatoes
2 oz. ($\frac{1}{4}$ cup) butter
1 pint ($2\frac{2}{3}$ cups) chicken stock
seasoning
1 oz. ($\frac{1}{4}$ cup) flour

$\frac{1}{2}$ pint ($1\frac{1}{3}$ cups) milk
1 large carrot
2 tablespoons chopped fresh herbs,
  or pinch dried herbs
$\frac{1}{2}$ pint ($1\frac{1}{3}$ cups) soured cream

Chop the onions and potatoes. Toss in the hot butter for a few minutes, take care the vegetables do not brown. Add the stock and simmer gently for 30 minutes. Season lightly. Sieve or emulsify the soup and return to the pan. Blend the flour with the milk and stir into the vegetable purée. Continue stirring over a low heat until the mixture thickens. Add the finely grated carrot, herbs, half the soured cream, and a little extra seasoning. Simmer for 5–10 minutes. Do not boil. Top with the remainder of the soured cream.
Serves 6–8.

Variations:
Add small sprigs cooked cauliflower after sieving.
Add thin cream and lemon juice to the soup instead of soured cream.
Creamed Borscht: Grate a medium sized cooked beetroot and add to the soup with the grated carrot, etc.
Chicken Chambertin: Add a little finely diced cooked chicken to the soup with the grated carrot, etc.

Economy hint:
Simmer the carcass of a chicken to produce really first class chicken stock. Use unsweetened evaporated milk and lemon juice instead of soured cream.

To prepare in advance:
Prepare the soup to the stage before adding the carrot, etc. Grate the carrot and keep in a polythene bag in the refrigerator. Continue heating as the recipe, but in the top of a double saucepan or basin over hot, but not boiling, water.

Following page: CHICKEN CHOWDER

Choosing Fish Dishes

When entertaining choose fish dishes that do not dry out if they are kept waiting for a while. It is always slightly difficult to plan exactly the cooking period, as your guests may be delayed and the meal will need to be later.

Fish dishes in a sauce are a wise choice for they can be prepared beforehand and simply reheated in the oven; do not over-cook the fish before putting it into the sauce, see Scalloped Fish on page 35.

Although fried fish is generally cooked at the last minute I find I can fry it until crisp and pale golden earlier in the day, then arrange it on absorbent paper on oven-proof dishes – spread the fish out so it will have a chance to re-crisp in the oven. Heat through again in the oven in time for the meal.

The Fritto Misto, page 35 is much more interesting than frying just one kind of fish, and is extremely economical because you can mix cheaper and more expensive kinds of fish.

Cold fish dishes are ideal, either as a first or main course, and the chaudfroid coating makes certain the fish remains moist in texture and looks most inviting; see the ideas on page 31.

Cold fish needs a good mayonnaise, see page 34.

One of the simplest ways to cook fish is to poach it in the oven in white wine with chopped fresh herbs to flavour. Season lightly, then serve the fish straight from the unthickened liquid. Trout, sole and mackerel are particularly good served in this way

If planning an informal or barbecue party then try kebabs of fish. Choose a firm fleshed fish, e.g. cod, hake, halibut, turbot. Cut the uncooked fish into neat cubes and put on to metal skewers with small mushrooms, small tomatoes and bacon rolls. Brush with melted butter, flavoured with seasoning and a little lemon juice, and grill or barbecue until tender.

Previous page: CRÈME CHAMBERTIN

Chaudfroid of Fish

This creamy coating can be used on cooked salmon, salmon trout, or even fillets of sole or plaice, although the latter are less inviting in a cold salad. Do not over-cook fish if serving this as a cold dish, for the fish continues to soften as it cools.

Chaudfroid Sauce for coating for 6–8 portions:
aspic jelly powder to set $\frac{1}{2}$ pint ($1\frac{1}{3}$ cups) water
1 level teaspoon powdered gelatine
$\frac{1}{2}$ pint ($1\frac{1}{3}$ cups) water

either $\frac{1}{2}$ pint ($1\frac{1}{3}$ cups) mayonnaise, see page 34 or $\frac{1}{2}$ pint ($1\frac{1}{3}$ cups) thick Béchamel sauce, see page 39
6–8 portions cooked fish
Garnish:
cucumber, etc.
lettuce
lemon

Mix the aspic jelly and powdered gelatine together, soften in a little cold water, then heat the remainder of the water and dissolve the softened aspic and powdered gelatine in this. Allow to cool, and then blend with the mayonnaise or the cool Béchamel sauce. Allow the mixture to stiffen very slightly. Arrange the pieces of fish on a wire cooling tray and coat with the Chaudfroid sauce. Press tiny pieces of cucumber, radish, pepper, tomato to form an attractive design on top of the sauce. When quite firm lift on to a bed of lettuce and garnish with lemon.
Serves 6–8.
Note: Put a large dish under the wire cooling tray, so any surplus sauce drops on to this.

Variation:
Chaudfroid mould of fish: Make the mixture as the coating above. When cool add approximately 1–$1\frac{1}{4}$ lb. well drained canned or cooked flaked fish – white fish, salmon, shell fish or use a mixture of fish. Put into an oiled mould and leave to set. Turn out on to a bed of mixed salad.

Trout Nansen

4 large trout or similar fish
little seasoning
$\frac{1}{2}$ pint ($1\frac{1}{3}$ cups) white wine, or
  use half wine and half water
$\frac{1}{4}$ pint ($\frac{2}{3}$ cup) fish stock*
bouquet garni
enough aspic jelly (jello) powder
  to set $\frac{1}{2}$ pint ($1\frac{1}{3}$ cups)
2–3 tablespoons thick mayonnaise
little chopped parsley

2–3 teaspoons chopped capers
1 tablespoon chopped gherkins
Garnish:
2 lemons
shelled prawns or shrimps,
  amount as required
2 skinned tomatoes
little cooked or canned asparagus
parsley

*Made by simmering the back bones for a short time or by simmering a small cod's head.

Slit the trout along the stomach and carefully remove the back-bones, or ask the fishmonger to do this. If using frozen trout allow to defrost, then bone. Try to leave the heads on the fish. Wash and dry the fish well. Season very lightly. Put into a large pan with the wine, or wine and water, and fish stock. Add the bouquet garni, but no more seasoning. Simmer very gently until tender, i.e. about 8–10 minutes. Lift the fish out of the liquid and drain well.

Strain the liquid most carefully, measure and if necessary add a little more wine or water to give just over $\frac{1}{2}$ pint ($1\frac{1}{3}$ cups). Soften the aspic jelly powder in a little of the liquid, heat the rest, then add the softened aspic jelly, stir until dissolved. Put on one side and leave until cool and beginning to stiffen. Meanwhile blend the mayonnaise, parsley, capers and gherkins and spread a little inside each fish. Put the fish on a serving dish with the sliced lemons, (serrate the edges of the lemons) and the prawns or shrimps. Peel the tomatoes, slice and cut one or two slices into small pieces, put these on the lemon rings. Arrange the rest of the sliced tomatoes and asparagus on the dish. Spoon the cold and slightly stiffened jelly over the fish and garnish, and leave until set. Top with parsley.
Serves 4.

Mayonnaise

2 egg yolks
$\frac{1}{2}$–1 teaspoon made English
   mustard or French mustard
$\frac{1}{4}$–$\frac{1}{2}$ teaspoon salt
good shake pepper
pinch sugar, optional

$\frac{1}{4}$ pint ($\frac{2}{3}$ cup) olive oil
1–2 tablespoons vinegar, white or
   brown malt or wine vinegar, or
   lemon juice
1 tablespoon boiling water,
   optional

Put the egg yolks, seasonings and sugar into a mixing bowl or basin. Beat well with a wooden spoon or with a whisk. Add the oil drop by drop, beating all the time. When the oil has been incorporated whisk in the vinegar or lemon juice. Taste once or twice to make sure you are not adding too much for your taste. Add the boiling water gradually at the end to give a very light creamy taste. Serve cold with salads.

To make a piping mayonnaise: add up to $\frac{1}{2}$ pint ($1\frac{1}{3}$ cups) oil; the more oil added the thicker the mayonnaise.

Mayonnaise in a liquidizer (blender):
Ingredients as above but the order of adding these is different. Put the egg yolks, seasonings and sugar into the liquidizer goblet, switch on for a few seconds. Add the vinegar or lemon juice. I would use the smaller amount the first time you make this. Switch on until blended. Switch to a low speed and pour the oil in very steadily. Taste and add any more vinegar or lemon juice required on low speed, then add the water.

Variations:
Green Mayonnaise: This is especially good with fish salads. Add freshly chopped herbs plus a little green colouring, or put a spinach leaf and the herbs into the liquidizer when the mayonnaise has thickened. Switch on until the herbs are chopped and the spinach blended. If making mayonnaise by hand chop the herbs finely, and add to mayonnaise.
Fennel Mayonnaise: Excellent with fish salads. Use chopped fennel leaves, or leaves plus a very little fennel root. Add to the mayonnaise.

34

Fritto Misto (Italian Fried Fish)

Buy the widest selection of fish possible, white fish of various kinds, shell fish – large prawns, mussels, scallops etc. In Italy they would use fresh anchovies or tiny fish, often mistaken for sardines, but really the fry of the shad. If you wish to provide variety to the dish, use well drained canned anchovy fillets and sardines.

$1\frac{1}{4}$ – $1\frac{1}{2}$ lb. mixed fish
Batter:
4 oz. (1 cup) flour, preferably
  plain
pinch salt

2 egg yolks
$\frac{1}{4}$ pint ($\frac{2}{3}$ cup) milk
2 tablespoons water
2 egg whites
little extra seasoned flour

Wash and dry the mixed fish. Make a batter with the flour, salt, egg yolks, milk, water and stiffly whisked egg whites. Coat the fish in a very little seasoned flour, then in the batter. Fry until the fish is crisp, golden brown and cooked. Drain on absorbent paper and serve with tomato or tartare sauce.
Serves 4–6.

Scalloped Fish

For a main course for 4 people (an hors d'oeuvre for 8) you would need $1\frac{1}{2}$–2 lb. fish – all white fish or a mixture of white fish, sliced scallops and prawns. Poach the fish in well seasoned milk, strain the liquid, then make a sauce with 2 oz. ($\frac{1}{4}$ cup) butter, 2 oz. ($\frac{1}{2}$ cup) flour, $\frac{1}{2}$ pint ($1\frac{1}{3}$ cups) white wine, and the cooking liquid, made up to $\frac{1}{2}$ pint ($1\frac{1}{3}$ cups) with milk. When thickened stir in 6 tablespoons thick cream and sliced fried mushrooms. Add the fish, top with buttered crumbs at once as this prevents a skin forming on the sauce. Heat gently in the oven and serve with lemon.

Following page: FRITTO MISTO

Fish Vol-Au-Vents

Scalloped Fish on page 35 would be ideal as a filling for vol-au-vent cases. The sauce must however be thicker so use only $\frac{3}{4}$ pint (2 cups) liquid. Add the fish, etc. to the sauce, blend in a very little thick cream.

If serving the vol-au-vents hot, warm the pastry in the oven, and the fish mixture in the top of a double saucepan or basin over hot water. Fill just before serving.

If serving the vol-au-vents cold, put the cold filling into the cold pastry.

Vol-Au-Vent Cases

Choose flaky pastry, rough puff pastry, or puff pastry. Roll out the pastry until about $\frac{1}{2}$-inch in thickness for fairly shallow cases or up to 1-inch for deep ones. Cut into required shape or shapes, i.e. either 1 large round or square, or a number of smaller shapes. Take a smaller cutter and press into the pastry; let it mark the pastry about half-way through. Bake a large vol-au-vent case in the centre of a hot to very hot oven, 450–475°F, Mark 7–8, for about 25–30 minutes, reduce the heat to very moderate, 325–350°F, Mark 3–4, after about 15 minutes. Small cases take from about 10 minutes (for cocktail size) to 15–20 minutes. Remove the pastry case or cases from the oven. Lift out the pastry lid very carefully. If you find there is a little uncooked mixture in the centre, return the cases to a very moderate oven, 325–350°F, Mark 3–4, until this is cooked.

If serving the vol-au-vent cases cold, then put the cold filling into the cold pastry. Place the lids in position, if wished. If serving hot, make quite sure both pastry and filling are very hot. Put together and serve at once.

Flaky or rough puff pastry made with 8 oz. (2 cups) flour, etc., will give 1 large vol-au-vent to serve about 6 people, 6–8 medium-sized cases or about 12–14 tiny ones. Puff pastry made with 8 oz. (2 cups) flour, etc., produces rather more vol-au-vent cases, since it rises more than the other pastries.

Previous page: VOL-AU-VENTS

Haddock Soufflé

Béchamel sauce:
piece carrot
piece celery
$\frac{1}{2}$ pint ($1\frac{1}{3}$ cups) milk
1 oz. butter
1 oz. ($\frac{1}{4}$ cup) flour

seasoning
8 oz. cooked fresh or smoked
  haddock
4 eggs

Put the carrot and celery in the milk. Warm gently for a few minutes then allow the pan to stand in a warm place for a time so the milk absorbs the flavour of the vegetables. Strain the milk. When making a coating Béchamel sauce measure the liquid and make up to $\frac{1}{2}$ pint ($1\frac{1}{3}$ cups) again. When using the Béchamel sauce for this soufflé or the Chaudfroid sauce, see page 31, then do not use any more milk.

Heat the butter in a large pan, stir in the flour, then cook for 2–3 minutes. Gradually work in the strained milk, bring to the boil and cook until thickened. Season well, add the flaked fish, the egg yolks, and then the stiffly whisked egg whites. Put into a greased soufflé dish and bake in the centre of a moderate oven, 350–375°F, Mark 4–5, for 35 minutes, until golden brown and well risen. Serve at once.

Serves 6 as an hors d'oeuvre or 3 as a light main course.

Variations:
Use about 6 oz. ($\frac{3}{4}$ cup) flaked cooked or canned tuna or salmon.
For a firmer textured soufflé use only $7\frac{1}{2}$ fluid oz. (barely 1 cup) milk for the Béchamel sauce.
A soufflé sinks less if you omit the egg yolks and use only the egg whites, so try this version, which serves a smaller number of portions, for parties.

To prepare in advance:
Make the sauce then leave it in the saucepan, and cover with damp greaseproof paper to prevent a skin forming. Prepare the fish.

Choosing Meat Dishes

Although meat dishes do not become over-cooked as readily as those made with fish, it is still wise to avoid methods of cooking where meat is ruined if your guests are a little late arriving for your party.

Roasted meat can be delayed by lowering the oven heat during cooking; and kept warm for some time with the oven turned low. Cover the joint with foil to prevent it becoming dry on the outside. Joints of meat take time to carve, so if you are expecting a number of guests you may be wiser to choose another type of meat cookery.

Meats may be grilled or fried as required, so there is no question of the meat spoiling. The only disadvantage is that you cannot leave the meat unattended, so that a hostess may find these troublesome methods of cooking.

A casserole of meat is an ideal party dish, for this can be prepared beforehand and left in the oven to cook; or it can be cooked beforehand and reheated – most casserole dishes taste better when warmed through after being cooked. Do not imagine that casseroles need to be dull in any way, the pages that follow give some suggestions. You can always alter the flavourings or vegetables used with the meat, to make a change. There are so many attractive oven-proof dishes available today that the cooking dish can also be the serving dish.

Highly spiced curries, etc. are excellent party dishes providing you are sure all your guests like these. If you are not certain then I would provide an alternative main course. Follow highly spiced dishes with a refreshing fruit-type dessert. The comments above apply to poultry dishes also.

RAGOUT OF BEEF AND PRUNES

Ragoût of Beef and Prunes

1 pint (2⅔ cups) brown stock
about 18 prunes
1¼ lb. chuck steak
seasoning
1 oz. (¼ cup) flour

2 oz. (¼ cup) cooking fat or
  dripping
1 tablespoon tomato purée
2 bay leaves
4–5 tomatoes

Heat the stock, pour over the prunes and soak for about 12 hours, unless using tenderized prunes which need soaking for 1 hour only. Dice the meat, roll in the seasoned flour and cook in the hot cooking fat or dripping for a few minutes. Strain the stock from the prunes, and add to the meat. Bring to the boil and cook until thickened. Add the tomato purée, about 6 finely chopped prunes and the bay leaves. Cover the pan and simmer for 1¾ hours. Add the rest of the prunes and cook for a further 15 minutes. Skin the tomatoes if wished, add to the ragoût and cook for 15 minutes.
Serves 4–5.

Variations:
The above recipe is both an economical and pleasant one and it can be altered in so many different ways.
Omit the prunes and use a few raisins instead; add these half way through the cooking so they do not become too soft.
Use dried apricots instead of dried prunes, soaking these in the same way as the prunes. When using apricots omit the tomato purée and flavour with the grated rind and juice of 1 lemon plus 2 teaspoons sugar.
Use ale instead of stock in the basic recipe.
Use chicken joints instead of beef and reduce the cooking time to 45 minutes instead of the 1¾ hours, then add the rest of the prunes and continue as the basic recipe. When cooking chicken use chicken stock or chicken stock mixed with white wine instead of brown stock.

Lamb Ratatouille

2 onions
1–2 cloves garlic
1½ lb. tomatoes
1–2 green peppers
1–2 aubergines (eggplants),
  optional
4 courgettes

8 lamb cutlets, or 2 lb. lamb from
  leg or shoulder
2 tablespoons oil
1–2 tablespoons chopped parsley
seasoning to taste

Peel and chop the onions, crush the garlic, skin and chop the
tomatoes, dice the peppers, discarding the core and seeds.
Slice the aubergines (eggplants) and courgettes thinly.
Fry the cutlets or cubed lamb in a pan for a few minutes on all
sides. Lift out, then add the oil. Toss the onion and garlic in
the oil for a few minutes then add the rest of the vegetables
and the parsley. Season very well. Cover the pan and simmer
for 25 minutes. Add the meat and blend with the vegetable
mixture so it absorbs the flavour. Cover the pan again. Cook
gently for a further 25–30 minutes.
Serves 8 for a light meal or 4–5 for a main meal.

Variations:
Beef Ratatouille: Use diced rump or topside instead of the
lamb.
Pork Ratatouille: This is an excellent way of cooking fairly
fat pork, for the vegetables absorb the surplus fat. Fry the
pork, as the lamb in the basic recipe, check how much fat has
run out, then adjust the amount of oil accordingly. Diced
bacon or ham may be used too, instead of the lamb.

Economy hint:
A small marrow may be used in place of the courgettes; when
aubergines (eggplants) are expensive, substitute small
mushrooms.

To prepare in advance:
Cook as the basic recipe for about 15 minutes, then put into
a casserole and heat gently for about 45 minutes in a very
moderate oven, 325–350°F, Mark 3–4.

Locro De Trigo (Argentine Beef Stew with Beans and Corn)

4 oz. (about $\frac{3}{4}$ cup) dried butter beans, soaked overnight, or use canned beans*

2 onions

1 large red pepper

$1\frac{1}{2}$ lb. chuck steak

2 tablespoons olive or other oil

2 pints ($5\frac{1}{3}$ cups) brown stock

2 teaspoons paprika

few bacon rashers**

8 oz. red or garlic sausage seasoning

about 8 oz. (just over 2 cups) canned or cooked sweet corn

*If using canned beans, drain and add with the sweet corn, you need a $1-1\frac{1}{4}$ lb. can.
**Green bacon if possible.

Drain the soaked beans, peel and chop the onions and dice the pepper, discarding the core and seeds. Cut the meat into small neat pieces. Heat the oil in a larger pan, toss the onion, pepper and beef in this for a few minutes. Blend the stock with the paprika, add this to the pan together with the butter beans, diced bacon, sliced sausage and seasoning. Bring the liquid just to boiling point, lower the heat, cover tightly and simmer gently for about 2 hours. Add the drained sweet corn and any extra seasoning desired. Simmer for a further 30 minutes.
This is a filling soup that makes a complete meal with bread.
Serves 6.

To prepare in advance:
Prepare the casserole completely with the exception of canned beans and corn which may be added when reheating.

Economy hint:
Garlic sausage is more expensive than Frankfurters, so slice these and use instead.

LOCRO DE TRIGO *(Photograph by Argentine Beef Bureau)*

Tajine Tfaia (Moroccan Lamb Dish)

$1\frac{1}{4}$–$1\frac{1}{2}$ lb. lean lamb – cut from
  the top of the leg if possible
good pinch cumin
pinch powdered saffron
pinch ginger
seasoning
finely grated rind 1–2 lemons
2 oz. ($\frac{1}{4}$ cup) butter

1–2 tablespoons oil
2 onions
1 clove garlic
little water or stock
about 1 tablespoon lemon juice
4 oz. ($\frac{4}{5}$ cup) blanched almonds

Cut the lamb into small cubes, about 1–$1\frac{1}{2}$-inches in size. Mix
the spices with seasoning and lemon rind and roll the meat in
this. Heat the butter and oil in a tajine or in a heat-proof dish,
or strong pan with a lid. Cook the lamb until it turns golden
brown on the outside. Add the finely chopped onions,
crushed garlic and just enough water or stock to prevent the
mixture becoming dry. Cover the cooking utensil and simmer
for about 10–15 minutes, until the meat and vegetables are
tender and moist – there should be no surplus liquid. Add
the lemon juice, any extra seasoning required and the
almonds. Heat for a few minutes and serve.
This is excellent with rice or the coarse semolina known as
cous-cous.
Serves 4–6.

Variation:
Use chicken instead of lamb. If the chicken joints are small do
not bone these. If preferred bone before cooking, then cut the
chicken into 1–$1\frac{1}{2}$-inch pieces. Since the dish looks whiter
with chicken you may wish to brown the blanched almonds
before adding to the mixture.

To prepare in advance:
The Tajine Tfaia – whether made with lamb or chicken – can
be cooked, and then warmed through gently in the oven.
Cook and rinse the rice, and warm on a flat dish, covering
with greased greaseproof paper so it does not dry.

Goulash of Gulyas
(Hungarian Paprika Stew)

12 oz. lean beef – choose good
  quality chuck steak
12 oz. stewing veal or lean pork
2–3 onions
2 oz. ($\frac{1}{4}$ cup) butter
seasoning

about 3 teaspoons paprika – use
  less the first time to make sure
  you enjoy the flavour
1–1$\frac{1}{2}$ lb. tomatoes
little water or white stock
Garnish:
soured cream
parsley

Cut the meat into neat pieces, peel and slice the onions neatly.
Heat the butter in a pan with a tightly fitting lid – this is
important for a goulash is a thick stew with little extra liquid.
Fry the meat in the hot butter until golden coloured, add the
onions, seasoning and paprika, and stir well to blend. Skin
and slice the tomatoes, put into the pan with a few tablespoons
water or stock. Cover the pan and simmer very gently until
the meat is tender. This will be about 1$\frac{1}{2}$–2 hours. If
necessary, add a little liquid during cooking. Turn into a
serving dish and top with soured cream and parsley.
Serve with boiled potatoes or noodles.
Serves 4–6.

Variations:
Sliced potatoes may be added half way through cooking.
Other meat or diced uncooked chicken may be used instead
of beef and veal.
This stew has a sweet, not a hot flavour, so most people would
enjoy it, even if they do not like curry.

To prepare in advance:
Either prepare beforehand and allow to cook for the time
given in the basic recipe in the centre of a very moderate
oven, 325–350°F, Mark 3–4, or cook and reheat.

47

Chicken Pilau

2 onions
1 clove garlic, optional
2 tablespoons chicken fat or oil
8 oz. (1¼ cups) long grain rice
1 pint (2⅔ cups) chicken stock –
  made by simmering chicken
  carcass or giblets

1–2 oz. (up to ½ cup) sultanas
few pine or other nuts, optional
12 oz. (1½ cups) diced cooked
  chicken
seasoning
Garnish:
few nuts or crisp breadcrumbs

Peel and chop the onions, crush the garlic. Fry in the hot fat
or oil for a few minutes, and then add the rice, turning in the
fat or oil. Add the stock, bring to the boil, and stir; then
simmer in an open pan for about 10 minutes. Add the rest of
the ingredients and cook for a further 10–15 minutes until the
liquid has just been absorbed. Pile on to a hot dish and top
with the nuts or crumbs.
Serves 4–5.

Variations:
Use diced cooked lean lamb instead of chicken.
Use uncooked chicken in the basic recipe. Allow at least
1 lb. (2 cups) boned diced chicken. Fry this in the hot oil with
the onions and garlic, and then add the rice and proceed as
the basic recipe.
Use uncooked diced lamb in the basic recipe. The ideal meat
would be a thick slice, weighing 1¼ lb., from the top of the
leg. Dice the lamb and fry with the onions and garlic. Add
the rice, etc. and proceed as the basic recipe, allowing about
20 minutes cooking time and increasing the amount of liquid
slightly.

To prepare in advance:
Prepare the dish as the basic recipe or one of the variations;
increase the amount of stock, for standing makes the rice
absorb more liquid. Simmer in an open pan as the basic
recipe, then transfer either to a casserole or the top of a
double saucepan. Add the rest of the ingredients and cook
gently for about 25–30 minutes.

Paprikascsirke
(Hungarian Paprika Chicken)

1 chicken
1 onion
little grated lemon rind
1½ pints (4 cups) water
4–5 peppercorns
little salt
bouquet garni

Sauce:
3 oz. (⅜ cup) butter
4 oz. (1 cup) button mushrooms
1 oz. (¼ cup) flour
1–2 tablespoons paprika
1 pint (2⅔ cups) stock, see method
¼ pint (⅔ cup) thick cream
seasoning

Joint the chicken – or buy 4 joints of chicken. Chop the onion. Put the lemon rind, chicken, water and onion into a pan with the peppercorns, salt and bouquet garni. Simmer until the chicken is tender. This takes about 45 minutes to 1 hour if young. Lift the chicken from the stock, strain the stock and keep 1 pint (2⅔ cups) for the sauce. Either dice the chicken or keep in the 4 joints.

Heat the butter in a pan. Toss the mushrooms in the hot butter for a few minutes, lift out on to a plate. Add the flour and paprika, stir well for 2–3 minutes over a low heat, then gradually blend in the stock, bring to the boil and cook, stirring, until thickened. Put the pieces or joints of chicken and mushrooms into the sauce. Simmer until thoroughly heated. Add some of the cream and seasoning, and simmer for 4–5 minutes; do not boil. Top with the remainder of the cream.

Serves 4–6.

Variations:
Although this particular recipe is more suited to chicken than other meats you could substitute diced veal or diced very young lean pork. The cooking time should be slightly longer for these meats.

To prepare in advance:
If cooking beforehand, take particular care not to over-cook the chicken.

Sweet Curry

2 medium-sized onions
1–2 cloves garlic
2 oz. ($\frac{1}{4}$ cup) cooking fat, butter
  or ghee*
1 small sweet apple
1–2 grated carrots
1 medium sized can pineapple,
  guavas or mangoes
$\frac{1}{2}$–1 tablespoon curry powder
$\frac{1}{2}$–1 tablespoon curry paste
1 tablespoon flour
$\frac{1}{2}$ pint ($1\frac{1}{3}$ cups) brown stock
1–2 tablespoons desiccated
  coconut, or grated fresh coconut
1–2 tablespoons sultanas
1–2 tablespoons chutney

1–$1\frac{1}{4}$ lb. uncooked beef, see
  method
1 teaspoon sugar
1 teaspoon lemon juice or vinegar
seasoning
Accompaniments:
6–8 oz. (1–$1\frac{1}{4}$ cups) long grain rice
saffron powder, optional
chutney
sliced peppers and tomatoes
Poppadums
Bombay duck
nuts
raisins
grated coconut
sliced banana
rings of raw onion or spring onions

*Ghee is clarified butter.

Chop the peeled onions and crush the cloves of garlic. Toss in
the hot fat. Peel and slice the apple, add to the onion mixture
with the carrots and most of the other fruit and the curry
powder and paste, and flour. Fry gently for several minutes,
stirring well to prevent the mixture burning. Gradually blend
in the stock and $\frac{1}{4}$ pint ($\frac{2}{3}$ cup) syrup from the can of fruit,
and bring to the boil; cook until slightly thickened. Put the
coconut, sultanas and chutney into the sauce, then add the
diced meat.
For special occasions choose diced topside, rump or fresh
brisket; for economy choose diced chuck or flank steak.
Simmer for about 1 hour in a tightly covered pan then add
the sugar, lemon juice or vinegar and seasoning. Taste the
sauce and add more sweetening or seasoning as desired. Cover
the pan again and continue cooking for a further $1\frac{1}{2}$–2 hours.
To cook the rice put this with about $2\frac{1}{2}$ times the amount of
cold water, i.e. to 8 oz. rice use 20 fluid oz. – 1 pint ($2\frac{2}{3}$ cups)
water; to 1 cup rice use $2\frac{1}{2}$ cups water. Add seasoning and a

pinch saffron powder if desired. Bring to the boil, stir briskly, cover the pan tightly and allow to simmer for approximately 15 minutes or until the rice has absorbed the water and is tender.

Arrange the curry in a border of saffron or plain rice or serve the rice in a separate dish. Garnish the curry with the remaining pieces of fruit just before serving. Arrange all the accompaniments in dishes so everyone may help themselves. The Poppadums should be fried in a very little fat until crisp. The Bombay duck, which is a dried fish, should be sprinkled over each portion of curry.

Serves 4–6.

Variations:

The curry sauce, see the basic recipe, is a good basic one. You can adjust this by omitting the pineapple or other fruit; by substituting water or white stock for the brown stock and by increasing or decreasing the amounts of curry powder and curry paste.

Make this sauce and use it to curry fish, chicken, etc.

To prepare in advance:

A curry sauce is far better if it is prepared and cooked the day before being required. It can be prepared, cooked and frozen very successfully too.

The uncooked meat or fish may be put into the sauce, then cooked on the following day. In this way it becomes impregnated with the curry flavour.

The rice may be cooked lightly, rinsed in cold water, then spread on to flat oven-proof dishes, covered with greased greaseproof paper and warmed in the coolest part of the oven, or it can be warmed in a covered basin over boiling water.

If you cook the curry in a covered casserole, after making the sauce, etc., it needs no attention.

Oriental Chicken

1 large roasting chicken*
Stuffing and sauce:
small can bean sprouts
4 oz. lean ham
small can water chestnuts
2 oz. ($\frac{1}{2}$ cup) chopped nuts
seasoning

2 tablespoons chopped preserved
  ginger
$\frac{3}{4}$ pint (2 cups) chicken stock
2 level tablespoons cornflour
2 tablespoons sherry
little oil

*A boiling fowl is unsuitable for this particular dish.

Wash and dry the chicken. Drain the bean sprouts, mix half with the diced ham. Drain and chop half the water chestnuts and add to the ham and bean sprouts, together with the chopped nuts, seasoning and half the ginger. Stuff the chicken with this mixture.

Blend the stock with the cornflour. Put into a pan and heat until thickened, stirring well. Add the remainder of the bean sprouts, sliced water chestnuts and ginger, together with a little seasoning and sherry. Pour this mixture into a large casserole. Place the chicken in the casserole. Brush the breast of the bird with oil and cover the casserole with a lid. Cook for 2 hours in the centre of a very moderate to moderate oven, 325–350°F, Mark 3–4.

Serves 6–8.

Variation:

Although the chicken looks much more impressive stuffed and served whole, it is more difficult to serve. You may care to make the stuffing as the basic recipe, then put this into a covered dish and cook it for about 1 hour in the centre of a very moderate oven, 325–350°F, Mark 3–4. Put 6–8 chicken joints, browned in a little oil, on top of the bean sprout mixture in the casserole and cook in a very moderate oven for 1 hour only.

Either spoon the stuffing round the edge of the casserole before serving or put the same dish on to the table.

To prepare in advance:

Prepare the sauce and stuffing beforehand, do not cook the chicken and reheat it.

54

Creamed Turkey Duchesse

1–1¼ lb. (2–2½ cups) mashed
  potatoes
2 eggs or 2 egg yolks
2 oz. (¼ cup) butter or margarine
seasoning
4 oz. (1 cup) button mushrooms
1 green pepper
½ pint (1⅓ cups) turkey stock,
  made by simmering the carcass
  or giblets
1 oz. (¼ cup) flour

¼ pint (⅔ cup) milk
few drops Tabasco sauce
about 1 lb. (2 cups) diced cooked
  turkey plus any small pieces of
  stuffing, optional
2–3 tablespoons top of the milk or
  thin cream
Garnish:
parsley

Blend the mashed potatoes with 1 egg or egg yolk and half the
butter or margarine; season well. Form into a border round
the edge of an oven-proof dish. Brush with the second egg or
egg yolk, diluted with a few drops of water, and brown in a
moderate oven, 350–375°F, Mark 4–5.
Meanwhile simmer the mushrooms and diced green pepper,
discarding the core and seeds, in the stock for 10 minutes.
Strain the liquid from the mushrooms and pepper, put this
on one side for the sauce. Heat the remainder of the butter or
margarine in a saucepan, stir in the flour, cook for several
minutes, stirring all the time, add the milk gradually, then the
stock. Bring to the boil, and cook until thickened, stirring
briskly, season well. Flavour with the Tabasco sauce. Taste
and add a little more Tabasco sauce, if desired. Put the
vegetables and turkey into the sauce and heat gently for a
few minutes. Add the stuffing and cream towards the end of
the heating period.
Bring the dish out of the oven. Pile the turkey mixture into
the centre and garnish with parsley.
Serves 4–6.

Variation:
Cooked pheasant or chicken may be used instead of turkey. If
using pheasant, simmer 1–2 diced onions in the stock to give
more flavour.

Hare in Madeira Sauce

1 jointed young hare
$\frac{1}{2}$ oz. flour
little chopped sage
3 oz. ($\frac{3}{8}$ cup) butter or cooking fat
4 oz. (1 cup) button mushrooms

12 tablespoons (1 cup) Madeira
  wine
good pinch dried or $\frac{1}{2}$ teaspoon
  freshly chopped herbs
seasoning

If wishing to serve 4 people only, use just the saddle of the
hare. If wishing to serve up to 8 people, use all the hare and
double all the ingredients in the recipe.
Sprinkle the saddle joints of hare with flour, mixed with a
little chopped sage. Heat half the butter or cooking fat and
brown the hare in this. Lift out of the pan and put into a
casserole. Heat the rest of the butter or cooking fat and cook
the mushrooms in this. Add to the casserole with the wine,
herbs and seasoning. Cover the casserole. Allow 1 hour in a
moderate to moderately hot oven, 375–400°F, Mark 5–6.
Serves 4.

Variations:
Make sage and onion stuffing a little stiffer than the recipe on
page 63, form into balls, and bake for a short time, then serve
with the hare; or make the stuffing exactly as the recipe on
page 63, bake separately and serve with the hare.

Casserole of Hare:
Simmer the liver of the hare to make a good flavoured stock.
Make a brown sauce with 3 oz. ($\frac{3}{8}$ cup) butter or dripping,
3 oz. ($\frac{3}{4}$ cup) flour, the stock, add seasoning, 2 tablespoons
red currant jelly and $\frac{1}{4}$ pint ($\frac{2}{3}$ cup) red wine. Fry the whole
jointed hare in a little cooking fat, drain, then fry 12 small
onions. Put the hare and onions into a casserole, top with the
sauce and cover, then cook for about 3 hours in a very
moderate oven, 325–350°F, Mark 3–4.

HARE IN MADEIRA SAUCE

Roast Chicken and Turkey

A large roasting fowl or capon serves 6–8. A medium-sized chicken can be cut into 4 portions and small spring chickens halved, or if very small, left whole as a portion for one. Guinea fowl is cooked and served as chicken. When buying turkey, remember there is a considerable weight of bone, so allow at least 12 oz. per person, i.e. a 12 lb. bird, weight when trussed, would provide portions for 14–16 people.

These are dry-fleshed birds and must be kept moist during cooking, so cover the bird, particularly the breast, with a generous amount of fat bacon or fat. Put stuffing inside the bird as it helps to keep it moist. Always weigh the bird after stuffing to calculate the cooking time. Baste the bird from time to time to keep it moist.

Timing:

Set the oven to hot, 425–450°F, Mark 7–8, the heat may be reduced to moderately hot, 375–400°F, Mark 5–6, after 15 minutes if roasting a small chicken and 30 minutes for a larger bird.

15 minutes per lb. and 15 minutes over for a bird up to 12 lb. in weight. After this add an additional 12 minutes per lb. up to 21 lb., and after this allow only 10 minutes for each additional 1 lb. If the bird is exceptionally broad-breasted be a little generous with the cooking time.

Bread Sauce

Bread Sauce:

This is a slightly richer recipe than often given, but it is much nicer. Put 3 oz. (1½ cups) soft breadcrumbs into a pan with ½ pint (1⅓ cups) milk, ½ oz. butter, 1 onion (stuck with 2–3 cloves), seasoning and 2 tablespoons thick cream. Heat very slowly until thickened and keep in a warm place until ready to serve. I generally put this into the top of a double saucepan over boiling water then it cannot burn. Remove the onion and cloves, and stir well before serving.

Serving Roast Poultry

Carving:
You may prefer to carve or joint the birds and serve each person at the table. Use a sharp knife or knives for carving, and poultry scissors if preferred for jointing chickens or duck. The easiest way to carve larger chickens, turkey and goose is to ease the leg away from one side of the bird, then carve slices from the breast and from this leg.

To prepare in advance:
If you wish to carve or joint the poultry early do this only just before the meal, so it does not become dry. Make sure the serving dish is very hot. Cover carved chicken or turkey with foil, so the flesh does not become dry.
Put sliced goose or jointed duck with the cut side downwards; arrange the crisp skin over the meat. Do not cover otherwise you lose the crispness of the skin.
Serve sage and onion or chestnut stuffing with duck or goose; parsley and thyme and chestnut stuffing with chicken or turkey; apple or orange sauce with duck or goose, and cranberry or bread sauce with chicken or turkey.

Parsley and Thyme Stuffing

Blend together 4 oz. (2 cups) soft breadcrumbs, 1–2 tablespoons chopped parsley, 2 oz. ($\frac{2}{5}$ cup) shredded suet, or melted margarine or butter, or chicken or turkey fat, 1–2 teaspoons chopped fresh thyme or good pinch dried thyme, grated rind and juice of 1 lemon and 1 egg. Season well.

Cranberry Sauce

Make a syrup of $\frac{1}{4}$ pint ($\frac{2}{3}$ cup) water and 2–3 oz. ($\frac{1}{4}$–$\frac{3}{8}$ cup) sugar. Add 8 oz. cranberries and 2 oz. ($\frac{1}{2}$ cup) sultanas and cook until tender. Add 1 tablespoon port wine if wished. The sauce can be put into the liquidizer goblet and emulsified.

Casserole of Duck

1 large duck
stuffing, see method
about 12 very small onions
1–2 cloves garlic
4–5 carrots
$\frac{3}{4}$ pint (2 cups) duck stock, made
  by simmering giblets

seasoning
1 oz. ($\frac{1}{4}$ cup) flour
4 large potatoes
Garnish:
parsley

This is an excellent way of cooking a rather fat duck. The
duck can be stuffed with sage and onion or chestnut stuffing
(pages 63 and 62), or with whole peeled apples and soaked,
but not cooked, prunes. Roast the duck in a hot oven,
425–450°F, Mark 7–8, for about 30 minutes, until really
crisp and brown and until much of the fat has run out.
While the duck is cooking, simmer the peeled onions, crushed
garlic and halved or quartered carrots in $\frac{1}{2}$ pint ($1\frac{1}{3}$ cups)
stock for 30 minutes, season well. Blend the flour with the
remaining stock, stir into the pan, and then cook until a
smooth thickened sauce. Transfer to a casserole with the
peeled and roughly sliced potatoes. Place the duck on top,
cover the casserole and cook for $1\frac{1}{2}$ hours in the centre of a
very moderate to moderate oven, 325–350°F, Mark 3–4.
Garnish with parsley.
Serves 4.
Variations:
Omit the carrots and potatoes and add about 8 oz. whole
peeled chestnuts and 12 soaked, but not cooked, prunes.
Duck in Honey and Chestnut Sauce: Omit the small onions
but add 1–2 whole onions to the liquid when simmering the
giblets. Strain this and make the sauce as the basic recipe, but
omit the carrots and potatoes. Stir 2 tablespoons honey and
1 tablespoon tomato purée into the sauce, together with
8–12 oz. peeled whole chestnuts. Proceed as the basic recipe.
To prepare in advance:
Crisp and brown the duck as the basic recipe. Make the sauce.
Transfer sauce and duck, etc. to the casserole and cook as the
recipe when required.

Roast Duck or Goose

Duck and goose are birds that contain a high percentage of fat. I find I obtain a really 'fat free' bird, with deliciously crisp skin if I cook the bird for about 30 minutes and take the roasting tin out of the oven. I then prick the skin carefully, but not too deeply, with a fine skewer and the excess fat spurts out. I do this once or twice for duck but at least twice more for a goose. I do not add any extra fat when cooking duck or goose. The cooking times are the same as for chicken and turkey, see page 58.

A large duck can be cut into 4 joints, but a small duckling should be halved.

Goose is a very extravagant bird, for it has very large bones and relatively little meat, so you should allow at least 1 lb. weight per person, after the bird is trussed.

The traditional accompaniments for both birds are apple sauce and sage and onion stuffing, see below and opposite, with thickened gravy. Orange sauce has become extremely popular during the past years and the recipe for this is opposite.

Apple Sauce

Simmer peeled sliced apples in a very little water until soft, sieve or beat until smooth or emulsify in the liquidizer, sweeten to taste.

This is particularly good if chopped cooked prunes and cinnamon are added to the sauce just before serving.

Chestnut Stuffing

Slit 1 lb. chestnuts and boil in water for 5–10 minutes, remove the skins while still warm. Put the chestnuts into $\frac{1}{2}$ pint ($1\frac{1}{3}$ cups) chicken, ham or turkey stock and simmer until tender and nearly all the stock is absorbed, then chop or sieve. Blend with 4 oz. ($\frac{1}{2}$ cup) diced ham, 8 oz. (1 cup) pork sausagemeat, seasoning and a little stock. If preferred, the chestnuts may be left whole.

Sage and Onion Stuffing

Peel, chop and cook 2–3 large onions for 10 minutes in $\frac{1}{4}$ pint ($\frac{2}{3}$ cup) water, season well. Strain, and then blend with 3 oz. ($1\frac{1}{2}$ cups) soft breadcrumbs, 1–2 teaspoons chopped fresh sage or $\frac{1}{2}$ teaspoon dried sage and 2 oz. ($\frac{2}{5}$ cup) shredded suet or melted margarine. Bind with the onion stock and/or an egg.

Orange (Bigarade) Sauce

$\frac{3}{4}$ pint (2 cups) duck stock made
  by simmering the giblets
2 large oranges*
$\frac{1}{2}$ oz. ($\frac{1}{8}$ cup) cornflour or
  arrowroot

2–3 teaspoons sugar
seasoning
2 tablespoons sherry or port wine,
  optional

*If you enjoy a bitter flavour choose Seville or bitter oranges rather than sweet oranges.

Strain the giblet stock very well. Grate or pare the rind, minus the white pith, from the oranges and simmer with the stock for about 10 minutes, no more. Strain carefully. Blend the orange juice with the cornflour or arrowroot, stir into the liquid and stir until clear. Allow the sauce to simmer gently until thickened. This takes quite a time, but improves the flavour. Add the sugar and seasoning, sherry or port wine and simmer again for a short time.
Serves 4–6.
Variations:
Richer Sauce: Blend in 1 oz. butter or well clarified duck fat.
With orange strips: Cut the rind, minus the white pith, of the oranges into matchsticks. Soak in the duck stock for 1 hour, simmer gently until tender, proceed as recipe.
Sweeter orange sauce: Blend 1–2 tablespoons red currant or apple jelly with the sauce. Omit or reduce the sugar.
An ordinary brown gravy made with giblet stock, etc. may be flavoured with a little orange juice and/or simmer pieces of orange rind, minus the white pith, in the gravy and strain.

Ham En Croûte

Joint middle gammon or ham, about 3½–4 lb.
1 lb. (4 cups) flour, preferably plain
pinch salt

8 oz. (1 cup) fat*
water to mix
Glaze:
1 egg

*See short crust pastry on page 102.

Soak the gammon or ham for 12 hours in cold water unless green or sweet-cure. If very salty soak for 24 hours. Lift out of the water, dry thoroughly and cut away the skin.
Sieve the flour and salt, rub in the fat until the mixture is like fine breadcrumbs. Mix with cold water to a rolling consistency. Roll out to about $\frac{3}{4}$ inch in thickness and cut off 2/3 of the pastry. Place the gammon or ham on the larger piece pastry, and bring up the pastry to encase the sides of the meat. Roll out the remaining pastry for the lid and place over the meat. Cut away any surplus pastry, brush the edges with beaten egg and pinch together very firmly. Lift on to a baking tray. Brush with beaten egg. Cut a slit in the top to allow the steam to escape. Make small leaves of pastry for decoration and press on top of the croûte and brush with beaten egg. Bake in the centre of a moderate oven, 350–375°F, Mark 4–5, for 30 minutes, then reduce the heat to very moderate, 325–350°F, Mark 3–4, for the remainder of the time. Allow 25 minutes per lb. and 25 minutes over, so a 4-lb. joint will take 2 hours 5 minutes. Serve hot or cold, cut into thin slices.
Serves 8–10.

Variations:
The recipe above gives a wonderful flavour to the ham, but the pastry is very well cooked and very crisp. If you want the pastry to be less hard, partially cook the ham by simmering gently, drain and dry well, then wrap in the pastry and continue cooking.
Joints of meat may be cooked in the same way as ham, the most successful being lean beef or leg of lamb.

HAM EN CROÛTE *(Photograph by RHM Foods Ltd)*

Cold Meat Dishes

There are many ways in which one can serve cold meats and cold poultry for a party.

Platter Anglaise:
This is the term given to a selection of cold meats. I would have some or all of the following if you have a large number of guests:
a) a small selection of salami of various types.
b) cold beef, either fresh or salted.
c) sliced ham en croûte, see page 65, or cold boiled ham or boiled gammon.
d) cold duck, garnished with orange slices, and/or cold chicken.
e) cold sliced tongue.
Serve various chutneys or pickles with these meats and poultry and a mixed salad, and garnish the large platter with small bunches of grapes as well as salad ingredients.

Chaudfroid of Chicken:
Cooked chicken joints may be coated with the same sauce as suggested under fish, see page 31. Use chicken stock to dissolve the aspic.

Chicken Vol-au-Vents:
Make the vol-au-vent cases as on page 38. Dice the chicken and mix this either with mayonnaise, blended with a little well seasoned cream, or with mayonnaise and soured cream or yogurt. If preferred make a Béchamel sauce as the recipe on page 39, using half milk and half chicken stock and keeping it a fairly thick consistency. Add diced chicken and just a little mayonnaise to the sauce. Spoon into the cold pastry cases just before serving. Garnish with paprika and parsley.

Aspic Mould:
Make up aspic jelly as the packet instructions – you can use

meat or chicken stock instead of water, but be careful it is not too salty. Allow the aspic jelly to cool and then blend with diced cooked meats and/or chicken and spoon into an oiled mould to set.

Choosing Vegetable Dishes

Cooked vegetables can be spoiled more easily than any other foods by over-cooking or by being kept waiting for too long a period. On the other hand one wants to avoid too much last minute dishing up, and straining vegetables can be a nuisance. If you can complete the cooking in the oven and reduce the heat well before the meal then the vegetables may be kept hot in the oven, with the heat turned very low. The vegetables may also be kept hot on a warming plate, or by standing the vegetable dishes over pans of hot, but not boiling, water. Always toss the vegetables in plenty of margarine or butter, so they do not dry out while being kept standing.

Aim to under-cook the vegetables slightly, as they will be just perfect when the time comes to serve them.

The following ideas may help you plan the vegetable course:

Ratatouille:
This is almost a perfect vegetable dish when you entertain. It is sufficiently moist to make a sauce unnecessary and it improves by standing a certain time.

Courgettes à la Provençale:
A similar type of dish to Ratatouille, this also improves by standing for a short period.

Cauliflower and Broccoli:
Coat with sauce to keep moist, or top with melted butter and chopped parsley or chives.

Peas and Beans:
Toss in plenty of butter and a layer of fried onion rings, which help to keep the vegetables moist.

Potatoes:
Make Duchesse potatoes by beating a generous amount of butter or margarine and egg yolks into the mashed potatoes, but do not add milk, then pipe or pile neatly into an oven-proof dish, brush with egg white and brown in the oven. These can be prepared well beforehand. They also freeze well.

Scalloped Potatoes:
Cut skinned or peeled potatoes into very thin slices. Put into an oven-proof dish with seasoning, melted butter or margarine and milk to cover. Cook steadily until tender and the milk is absorbed – about $1\frac{1}{4}$ hours in a very moderate to moderate heat, 325–350°F, Mark 3–4.

Onion à la King

about 24 tiny onions or shallots, or about 36 spring onions or scallions
seasoning
1 green pepper
4 eggs
1½ oz. butter or margarine
1½ oz. (⅜ cup) flour

¾ pint (2 cups) milk, or milk and onion stock
3–4 tablespoons cooked sweet corn
Croûtons:
2 slices bread
2 oz. (¼ cup) cooking fat or butter

Prepare the onions, cutting some of the stalk from spring onions or scallions, but leave about 1 inch green. Cook in well seasoned boiling water until just tender; do not over-cook. Cut the green pepper into narrow strips (discarding core and seeds) and add to the liquid for the last 5 minutes. Meanwhile boil the eggs until just firm, shell and slice. Make the white sauce with the butter or margarine, flour and milk or milk and onion stock. Add the sweet corn, sliced eggs and drained onions and pepper. Season well and serve topped with fried croûtons of bread. To make these, dice the bread and fry until crisp and brown in the hot cooking fat or butter. **Serves 4.**

Variations:
Celery à la King: Cook diced celery then prepare as the basic recipe or use canned celery hearts.
Freshly cooked asparagus may also be used in the same way and so can diced cauliflower or broccoli spears.
Onions Florentine: Prepare the onions as the recipe above. Cook and then strain the spinach. Put the spinach at the bottom of an oven-proof serving dish, top with the onion mixture. Omit the croûtons of bread. The onion sauce prevents the spinach drying out.

To prepare in advance:
Make the onion mixture, fry the croûtons and keep both warm in the oven. Tip the croûtons over the dish at the last minute.

Potatoes Dauphine

8 oz. (1 cup) sieved potatoes or
use instant potatoes and prepare
as instructions on the packet
seasoning
Choux pastry:
2 oz. ($\frac{1}{4}$ cup) butter

$\frac{1}{4}$ pint ($\frac{2}{3}$ cup) water
3 oz. ($\frac{3}{4}$ cup) flour, preferably plain
2 eggs plus 1 egg yolk
seasoning
deep oil or cooking fat for frying

Beat the sieved potatoes with seasoning until very smooth or
make up the instant potatoes.
Put the butter and water into a pan and heat until the butter
has melted. Remove the pan from the heat, add the flour and
stir over a low heat until the flour mixture forms a dry ball.
Gradually beat the eggs and egg yolk into the choux pastry
then blend in the potato purée. Taste, add more seasoning
if required.
Heat the oil or fat. To test this, drop in a cube of day-old
bread. If the temperature is correct it will turn golden brown
in just over 30 seconds. Either pipe or spoon small balls of the
mixture into the oil or fat and fry for a few minutes until
golden brown. Drain on absorbent paper, serve at once.
Serves 4–6.

Variations:
The above recipe gives a particularly light version. You can
use up to 1 lb. (2 cups) sieved potatoes to the amount of choux
pastry given.
Add 2–3 tablespoons finely grated cheese (Parmesan,
Gruyère, Cheddar) to the mixture, with or after adding the
potatoes. Flavour with chopped parsley and/or nutmeg.

To prepare in advance:
These cannot be kept hot for a very long period since they
lose their light crispness. It is better to prepare the potatoes,
then prepare the choux pastry, put the mixture together and
cook just before required.

POTATOES DAUPHINE
(Photograph by Cadbury Schweppes Food Advisory Service, Bournville, Birmingham.)

Ratatouille

1 medium-sized to large aubergine (eggplant)	1–2 cloves garlic
	1 green pepper
about 8 oz. courgettes	1 red pepper
seasoning	3–4 tablespoons olive oil
1 lb. ripe tomatoes	**Garnish:**
4 medium-sized onions	chopped or sprigged parsley, optional

If you dislike the taste of the peel on an aubergine (eggplant) remove this, otherwise dice the vegetable neatly with the peel on. Slice the courgettes. Put the vegetables into a bowl, sprinkle lightly with salt and pepper, leave for 30 minutes. This minimizes the bitter taste from the aubergine (eggplant) peel, and draws out the water from the courgettes. Skin and slice or chop the tomatoes and onions; chop or crush the cloves of garlic. Dice the flesh from the peppers, discarding the cores and seeds.

Heat the olive oil in a pan, add the tomatoes and onions and cook gently for a few minutes, to let the juice flow from the tomatoes. This makes sure the mixture will not stick to the pan. Add the rest of the vegetables, and stir well. Season and cover the pan with a tightly fitting lid. Simmer gently until as tender as you would wish, about 30 minutes in all. Serve hot.

If you wish this to be a cold hors d'oeuvre, then I suggest cooking them a little longer until quite soft. Top with parsley before serving.

Serves 6–8.

Variations:

The recipe uses the minimum of oil, you may prefer to use more. Add 3–4 tablespoons chopped parsley, or parsley and chives to the vegetables before cooking.

Cook in a tightly covered casserole for at least 45 minutes in a very moderate oven, 350–375°F, Mark 4–5, or 1 hour in a slow oven, 275–300°F, Mark 1–2.

The proportions of vegetables are entirely a matter of personal taste. Add sliced mushrooms if wished and omit the peppers.

Courgettes à la Provençale

1 lb. ripe tomatoes
1–2 cloves garlic
1 onion
little stock or water

1 lb. courgettes
seasoning

Skin and chop the tomatoes and put into the pan with the crushed garlic and very finely diced onion. Add a little stock, chicken for preference, or water, and simmer until a thin purée. Wipe and slice the courgettes thinly, add to the purée, with a generous amount of seasoning and simmer steadily for about 30 minutes until tender. If the purée of tomatoes seems too thin lift the lid of the pan, so excess liquid can evaporate, but watch that the mixture does not stick to the bottom of the pan.
Gives generous portions for 4.

Variation:
Richer version: Toss the sliced courgettes in a little oil before adding the crushed garlic and onion. Fry these also until the courgettes are very pale golden coloured, then add the tomatoes, stock or water and seasoning. This version makes a better hors d'oeuvre.

To prepare in advance:
Make either version and put into a casserole and heat through gently.

Economy hint:
Use diced marrow instead of the more expensive courgettes. When marrows etc. are very young there is no need to remove either the peel or the barely formed seeds.

New way to serve:
If you add diced bacon, fried until crisp, or diced cooked ham, chopped parsley and a little chopped lemon thyme this makes an excellent dressing for chicken and there is no need to make either a stuffing or a sauce.

Choosing Salads

There are no hard and fast rules about the ingredients that should be put into a salad. When entertaining, let any salad dish lend colour to the table, but above all let it blend and help to balance the rest of your menu. Remember, a refreshing green salad is ideal with rich dishes, such as roast duck, fish or meat or poultry in a rich sauce.

If the main dish is rather colourless, then this is an ideal opportunity to put as many colourful ingredients into a salad as possible, providing they blend in flavour. Choose contrasting textures as well as flavours.

A good dressing is essential to a good salad – the following French dressing can be adapted to suit not only personal taste, but the ingredients in the salad. If you have included citrus fruits then you need less lemon juice or vinegar. If you are serving the salad with a rather bland dish, then be generous with the lemon juice or vinegar.

French Dressing:
Blend olive or salad oil with a little made mustard, add seasoning and a pinch of sugar, then work in lemon juice or vinegar. Most people like about twice as much oil as lemon juice or vinegar. Taste and adjust seasoning, etc.

American Salad:
Mix cooked green beans, cooked or canned sweet corn, finely diced red pepper, sliced raw mushrooms, sliced firm tomatoes, and black olives. Toss in oil and vinegar. Put into a dish and top with rings of raw onion. Serve this salad with cold chicken or turkey and with most meats.

Choosing Desserts

A good dessert 'rounds off' a special occasion meal, so spend a little time thinking about your choice of sweet. Unless you have help in the kitchen choose a dessert that needs little if any last minute attention.

If the rest of the menu has been rather creamy and rich in flavour then base the dessert on the refreshing flavour of fresh fruit. One of the most popular and delicious is a fresh fruit salad. Simply blend a selection of seasonal fresh fruit together. Moisten the fruits with fresh orange juice or white wine, or Kirsch, or make a syrup of sugar and water and flavour this with lemon or orange juice. If preferred mix a little canned fruit with the fresh fruit and use the syrup from the can to moisten the fruit salad.

If the fruit salad contains fruits that discolour easily, i.e. bananas, apples, fresh peaches or pears, make sure they are covered by the syrup or juice. Put a small plate on top of the fruit salad, so you push the fruit under the liquid. In this way all fruits retain their colour without having too much liquid. Crisp fruit, such as apples, can be added later if wished so they do not soften.

Very few people dislike ice cream, particularly when it is made into an interesting sweet, as those on pages 82–87. Nowadays various gâteaux are served for desserts. Most of these have the advantage of being better if made a while before they are served, so there are no last minute preparations.

If you make good pastry then fruit pies could be your choice. Remember these can be baked beforehand and warmed through gently or served cold.

CREAM DESSERTS

Cream Flan

Flan case:
2 eggs
3 oz. ($\frac{3}{8}$ cup) castor sugar
2$\frac{1}{2}$ oz. (just over $\frac{1}{2}$ cup) flour,
 plain or self-raising

Filling:
$\frac{1}{2}$ pint (1$\frac{1}{3}$ cups) thick cream, or
 $\frac{1}{4}$ pint ($\frac{2}{3}$ cup) thick and $\frac{1}{4}$ pint
 ($\frac{2}{3}$ cup) thin cream
8–12 oz. fruit, raspberries,
 strawberries, passion fruit pulp,
 peaches, etc.
little sugar

Whisk the eggs and sugar until thick. Fold in the sieved flour. Grease and flour an 8–9-inch sponge flan tin. Spoon in the mixture and bake for about 12 minutes above the centre of a moderate to moderately hot oven, 375–400°F, Mark 5–6, until firm to the touch. Turn out carefully and leave until quite cold.

Whip the thick cream until it just holds a shape, or whip the thick cream then gradually whisk in the thin cream. Halve or mash most of the fruit and blend with the cream, add the sugar.

Lift the sponge flan on to a serving plate. Fill with the cream mixture and decorate with fruit. Serve with extra cream or ice cream.

Serves 5–6.

Variations:

Alaska Flan: Make the flan case as the recipe above then fill with fruit and very firm ice cream. Make a meringue with 3 egg whites and 3–6 oz. castor ($\frac{3}{8}$–$\frac{3}{4}$ cup) sugar. The quantity of sugar depends upon personal taste. Pile the meringue over the ice cream and flan, which should be on an oven-proof dish. Bake for about 3 minutes in a very hot oven, 450–500°F, Mark 8–10, until golden brown.

Note: You can use a base of bought cake or other cake instead of the sponge flan, or a square of baked puff pastry.

79

Crème Brûlée

Caramel:
3 tablespoons granulated or castor sugar – or equivalent in loaf sugar
3 tablespoons water
Custard:
$\frac{1}{2}$ pint ($1\frac{1}{3}$ cups) milk
4 eggs

1 tablespoon sugar
$\frac{1}{2}$ pint ($1\frac{1}{3}$ cups) thick cream
Topping:
2 tablespoons blanched almonds
2 tablespoons sieved icing sugar

To make the caramel put the sugar and water into a strong saucepan. Stir over a low heat until the sugar has dissolved. If the sugar and water splash against the sides of the saucepan brush with a pastry brush dipped in cold water. This helps to prevent the mixture crystallizing. Allow the sugar and water syrup to boil steadily until golden brown. Leave in the saucepan and cool slightly. Add the milk, heat gently until blended with the caramel. Beat the eggs with the sugar and cream, add the caramel and milk mixture.
Strain into an oven-proof or soufflé dish. This can either be a deep dish, or you can cook it in a shallow dish in which case you may like to use a little extra topping. Stand the dish in a bain-marie, i.e. another dish containing cold water, and bake in the coolest part of a slow oven, 275–300°F, Mark 1–2, for approximately 45 minutes to 1 hour until the mixture is set. Top with almonds and sugar and brown for a few minutes under the grill.
Serves 4–6.

Variation:
Allow the dessert to become cold again after putting under the grill and top with a border of piped cream.
Vienna Pudding: Crumble 4–8 oz. (2–4 cups) rich fruit cake into a basin. Make the custard mixture as the basic recipe or the economical variation. Cook as the basic recipe.

Economy hint:
Use all milk in the recipe, rather than milk and cream, or reduce the proportion of cream and increase the milk.

ICED DESSERTS
Basic Cream Ice

2 large eggs
2 oz. ($\frac{1}{4}-\frac{3}{8}$ cup) sugar*
$\frac{1}{4}$ pint ($\frac{2}{3}$ cup) thick cream

$\frac{1}{4}$ pint ($\frac{2}{3}$ cup) thin cream
flavouring

*Preferably icing sugar. Cup measure depends on sugar used.

Whisk the eggs and sugar until thick and creamy. Whip the thick cream until it just begins to hold its shape then gradually whisk in the thin cream. Add the flavouring required and fold into the egg mixture. Spoon into a freezing tray or other utensil and freeze until firm. This mixture does not need beating during freezing.

If using an electric mixer, whisk the eggs and sugar, pour the thick cream on to the beaten eggs and sugar, continue whisking until thick again. Then gradually whisk in the thin cream and flavouring. Freeze as above.

Serves 4 or 6 with other ingredients, such as fruit.

Variations:

For a whiter ice cream use the egg whites only. Whip these until very stiff and fold into the whipped cream.

For a more economical ice cream use the egg yolks to make a custard sauce with $\frac{1}{2}$ pint ($1\frac{1}{3}$ cups) milk and sugar. Cool, fold in the whipped cream, flavouring and finally the stiffly whisked egg whites.

Use $\frac{1}{2}$ pint ($1\frac{1}{3}$ cups) evaporated milk in place of the thick and thin cream. To whip evaporated milk boil the tin of milk in water for 15 minutes, cool then whisk until thick.

Flavourings for ice cream:

Add $\frac{1}{2}-1$ teaspoon vanilla or other essence.
Add $\frac{1}{2}-1$ tablespoon sweetened coffee essence.
Add $\frac{1}{2}-1$ oz. sieved cocoa.
Add $\frac{1}{4}-\frac{1}{2}$ pint ($\frac{2}{3}-1\frac{1}{3}$ cups) thick fruit purée. The most suitable fruits are raw sieved strawberries, raspberries and bananas, or cooked, sieved apricots, blackcurrants, gooseberries and damsons.

Apple Water Ice

1 lb. cooking apples
1 lemon
$\frac{1}{2}$ pint ($1\frac{1}{3}$ cups) water
4 oz. ($\frac{1}{2}$ cup) sugar

2 teaspoons powdered gelatine
colouring
1 egg white
Garnish:
mint leaves

Wash and chop the apples, do not remove peel or cores, as these give flavour. Put into a saucepan with the thinly pared lemon rind, water and sugar. Simmer until the apples are very soft. Sieve the mixture, return to the pan to keep warm. Soften the gelatine in the cold lemon juice, add to the warm apple mixture, and stir until dissolved. Taste, and add extra sugar as desired, or if the apples are rather sweet add a little more lemon juice. Tint the juice a delicate shade of green or pink. Cool, and then freeze. Pour into freezing trays or a deeper utensil. Freeze on the normal setting in the refrigerator or home freezer. Leave until lightly frosted. Remove and blend with the stiffly beaten egg white. Return to the freezing compartment or freezer and continue freezing. Serve in glasses, or pile into canned peach halves, and decorate with mint leaves. The combination of the sharp apple mixture and the sweet peach is delicious.
Serves 6, or 8 when served with other ingredients, such as peaches.
Variations:
Use other fruit in place of apples. Plums, damsons, rhubarb, gooseberries, etc., should be cooked. Raspberries, strawberries and other soft fruits should be used raw and blended with the syrup, made by heating the water, sugar and lemon rind. Two fruits can also be blended together.
To prepare in advance:
Water ices, like ice creams, are an excellent choice when planning ahead. Bring out of the freezing compartment or freezer a little while before serving. Pile into the peach halves then return to the freezer for a very short time, otherwise the peaches become too hard.

Pacific Delight

1 ripe medium-sized pineapple
ice cream to serve 4 or 6

Meringue:
4 egg whites
4 oz. ($\frac{1}{2}$ cup) castor sugar

Cut the top from the pineapple very carefully. Put this on one
side to be used for decoration. Cut the pineapple into 4 or 6
rings and then remove the skin from each slice with a sharp
knife or kitchen scissors. Take out the centre core with an
apple corer, or sharp knife. This can all be done well in
advance.
Make sure the ice cream is firm. Whisk the egg whites until
very stiff. Gradually whisk in half the sugar then fold in the
remainder.
Put the first slice of pineapple on to an oven-proof serving
dish. Fill the centre hole of the pineapple with ice cream. Top
with a second slice of fruit and ice cream, continue like this
until the fruit is put together. Put the meringue mixture into
a cloth piping bag with a $\frac{1}{4}$–inch rose, and pipe over the fruit
to look like the original shape of the pineapple. Put into a
very hot oven, 475–500°F, Mark 8–9, and leave for about
3 minutes only, until the meringue is tinged golden brown.
Remove from the oven. Put the pineapple leaves into position,
on the top of the meringue shape. Serve at once, or this
dessert will stand for about 25–30 minutes without the ice
cream melting.

Note: When fresh pineapple is not available, use rings of well
drained canned pineapple, in which case use a little less
sugar in the meringue.
There is another way to serve this dessert, and that is to peel
the pineapple and cut into slices downwards, removing the
hard core. Put a block of ice cream on to the dish, press the
slices against the ice cream so it looks like a whole pineapple
again, then coat with meringue as the recipe above.

Fruit Melba

One of the most delicious iced desserts is a Fruit Melba. In this fresh, well-drained canned, or thawed-out frozen fruits are arranged round an ice cream and then topped with Melba sauce, see below.

The most suitable fruits are: Strawberries and other berry fruits, pears, peaches, pineapple or apricots.

Coupe Jacques:

This is the name given to fruit salad, ice cream and a Melba sauce.

Poires Helene:

Arrange halved well-drained canned pears or fresh dessert pears round ice cream.

Top with hot or cold chocolate sauce, see recipe opposite.

Sundaes:

These may be made by arranging layers of fruit, whisked jelly and ice cream, or by coating ice cream with various sauces, chopped nuts, cream, etc.

Melba Sauce

8 oz. (1¾ cups) raspberries*
¼ pint (⅔ cup) water*
2 oz. (¼ cup) sugar

2 tablespoons redcurrant jelly
1 teaspoon cornflour or arrowroot

*If using canned or frozen raspberries use the syrup instead of water and reduce sugar if wished.

Put the raspberries, most of the water and the sugar into a pan with the redcurrant jelly. Heat gently, until the redcurrant jelly has dissolved. Blend the cornflour or arrowroot with the remainder of the water, stir into the raspberry mixture then cook until thick and clear. Sieve or emulsify.

Serves 4–6.

Chocolate Sauce

4–6 oz. plain chocolate or
   chocolate couverture
   (cooking chocolate)

1–2 tablespoons water
about $\frac{1}{2}$ oz. butter

Break the chocolate into pieces and put into a basin with the
water and butter. Use the larger amount of water if serving
the sauce cold. Heat over hot, but not boiling water.
Serves about 4 good portions.

Variations:
Economical Chocolate Sauce: Put 2 tablespoons water into
a saucepan with 1 tablespoon sugar, 1 tablespoon golden
syrup, 1 oz. butter or margarine and a few drops vanilla
essence. Heat for 2–3 minutes then blend in 2 level
tablespoons cocoa powder. Stir until well dissolved. Add a
little more water, if this sauce is being kept hot for any
length of time.
Mocha Sauce: Use strong made coffee instead of water in the
basic recipe or the variation. Excellent with coffee ice cream.
Chocolate Orange Sauce: Use orange juice instead of water
in the basic recipe or the variation. This is delicious with
fresh orange segments and ice cream.

To prepare in advance:
Keep the chocolate sauce hot over a pan of very hot water.
I generally remove the pan from the cooker so there is no
danger of the water boiling too fast.

Lemon Soufflé

finely grated rind of 2 lemons
4 tablespoons lemon juice
3 eggs
4–6 oz. ($\frac{1}{2}$–$\frac{3}{4}$ cup) castor sugar

$\frac{3}{4}$ tablespoon powdered gelatine
4 tablespoons water
$\frac{1}{2}$ pint (1$\frac{1}{3}$ cups) thick cream
Decoration:
small ratafia biscuits

Put the lemon rind, juice, egg yolks and sugar into a basin over a pan of very hot water. Whisk until thick and creamy. Soften the gelatine in the cold water, and add to the egg yolk mixture, stirring over the heat until the gelatine has dissolved. Cool and allow to stiffen slightly.

Whip the cream lightly, fold into the jellied mixture. Whisk the egg whites until stiff, but not too dry, fold into the mixture. Spoon into the prepared soufflé dish, see below. Allow to set and remove the paper slowly and carefully. Press some finely crushed ratafia biscuits on to the sides of the soufflé and decorate the top with ratafias.

Serves 5–6.

To prepare a soufflé dish:
Cut a band of greaseproof paper three times the depth of the dish. Fold the paper to give a double thickness, and brush the part that will stand above the dish with a very light coating of melted butter. Tie or pin the band of paper very securely round the outside of the soufflé dish.

Variations:
Use orange rind and juice instead of lemon rind and juice.
Use 6 tablespoons ($\frac{1}{2}$ cup) water plus 2 tablespoons crème de menthe or other liqueur in the recipe above, omitting the lemon rind and juice.
Use $\frac{1}{4}$ pint ($\frac{2}{3}$ cup) fruit purée instead of the lemon juice, and reduce the water to 2 tablespoons. Omit the lemon rind.
Omit the lemon rind and juice and add 3 oz. plain chocolate to the egg yolks, etc.

Syllabub

½ pint (1⅓ cups) thick cream
1–2 oz. sieved icing sugar

juice 1 lemon
up to ¼ pint (⅔ cup) white wine

Beat the cream as directed below, do not over-beat as you have to whisk in the other ingredients. Gradually whisk in the sugar, lemon juice and as much of the white wine as you desire. The mixture will be very soft. Spoon into glasses or small dishes and chill. Serve with fingers of sponge, cake or sweet biscuits.
Serves 4.

Variation:

Orange and Lemon Syllabub: Use lemon and orange juice, a total of about 5 tablespoons and omit the wine. Decorate with piped cream and small pieces of crystallized orange slices. This mixture is less soft than the basic recipe.

To whip fresh cream:
Put thick cream into a basin. Use an electric or hand whisk, or a fork to whip the cream. The latter is slow, but safer if the cream is very rich. Whip slowly and steadily until the cream begins to stand in peaks. This consistency is ideal when adding cream to desserts. If using the cream for piping, it should be stiffer and stand in peaks.

To make a lighter cream:
1. Whip as above, then fold in an equal quantity of thin cream. Whip again until it stiffens. This will be rarely firm enough to use for piping.
2. To each ¼ pint (⅔ cup) thick cream add one egg white. Whip the cream and egg white in separate basins and fold together just before serving. You can pipe this, although it tends to be much softer than thick cream alone.

CAKES AND GÂTEAUX

Orange Layer Cake

4 oz. ($\frac{1}{2}$ cup) margarine, butter or cooking fat (shortening)
4 oz. ($\frac{1}{2}$ cup) castor sugar
2 small eggs
2 tablespoons orange juice
5 oz. ($1\frac{1}{4}$ cups) self-raising flour, with plain flour use 1 teaspoon baking powder

Filling:
4 oz. ($\frac{1}{2}$ cup) butter or margarine

8 oz. ($1\frac{1}{2}$ cups) sieved icing sugar
grated rind 1 orange
little orange juice

Icing:
6 oz. ($1\frac{1}{8}$ cups) icing sugar
little orange juice
pink colouring
few crystallized orange slices
small pieces of angelica

Cream the margarine, butter or cooking fat with the sugar until soft and light in colour; use a wooden spoon for this. If using a mixer warm the bowl, but not the fat, to ease mixing. Gradually beat in the eggs and the orange juice, then fold in the sieved self-raising flour, or flour and baking powder, with a metal spoon. Divide the mixture between two 7-inch greased and floured sandwich tins.

Bake above the centre of a moderate oven, 350–375°F, Mark 4–5, for 15–20 minutes until just firm to the touch. Cool for 2–3 minutes in the tins. Turn out carefully. When the cakes are cool, split to give 4 layers.

Cream the butter or margarine and icing sugar, add the orange rind and enough juice to make the consistency of a thick whipped cream. Sandwich the cakes together with most of this. Top with the icing made by blending the icing sugar with enough orange juice to give a soft spreading consistency and 2 or 3 drops of colouring. When firm, pipe rosettes of the remaining butter icing and decorate with portions of crystallized orange slices and small pieces of angelica.

Gives about 6 good slices.

Coffee Walnut Layer Cake

6 oz. ($\frac{3}{4}$ cup) butter or margarine
6 oz. ($\frac{3}{4}$ cup) castor sugar*
3 large eggs
1 egg yolk
1 tablespoon strong coffee
6 oz. ($1\frac{1}{2}$ cup) self-raising flour,
  or preferably plain flour and
  1 level teaspoon baking powder
3 oz. ($\frac{3}{4}$ cup) finely chopped
  walnuts

Filling:
4 oz. ($\frac{1}{2}$ cup) butter
8 oz. ($1\frac{1}{2}$ cups) icing sugar
1 tablespoon milk
Frosting:
8 oz. (1 cup) granulated sugar
4 tablespoons water
pinch cream of tartar
1 egg white
few walnut halves

*You can also omit 1 oz. ($\frac{1}{8}$ cup) castor sugar and use the same amount of brown sugar, which gives a very pleasant flavour and colour to the cake.

Cream the butter or margarine and sugar until soft and light. Gradually beat in the eggs, egg yolk and coffee. Fold in the sieved self-raising flour or plain flour and baking powder and the chopped walnuts. Grease and flour two 7–8-inch sandwich tins, or line the bases with greased greaseproof paper. Divide the mixture between the tins and smooth flat on top. Bake just above the centre of a moderate oven, 350–375°F, Mark 4–5 for approximately 25 minutes, until firm to the touch. Turn out carefully, cool.
Cream the butter and icing sugar together, and add the milk. Split each cake through the centre to give four layers, spread with the butter icing and put the cake together again. Put the sugar and water into a strong saucepan, and stir until the sugar has dissolved. Boil steadily, without stirring, until the mixture reaches 238–240°F, i.e. it forms a 'soft ball' when tested in cold water. Add the pinch cream of tartar and beat hard until cloudy, then pour steadily on to the stiffly whisked egg white. Continue beating until the icing thickens, then spread over the top and sides of the cake. Decorate with walnut halves.
Makes 6–8 good slices.

Meringue Gâteau

4 egg whites
8 oz. (1 cup) castor sugar*

½ pint (1⅓ cups) thick cream
fresh or canned fruit
sugar or vanilla sugar, see below

*Or use half castor and half sieved icing sugar.

Whisk the egg whites until very stiff, then gradually whisk in half the sugar and fold in the remainder.
Brush 1 or 2 baking trays with a very little olive oil or melted butter, or cut out 3 or 4 rounds of greaseproof paper, put on the trays, then brush with oil or butter. Spread or pipe the meringue mixture on to the trays to give 3 or 4 rounds. 'Dry out' in the coolest part of a very slow oven, 225–250°F, Mark 0–½, for about 2 hours until crisp. Lift off the tins with a warm palette knife, store in an airtight tin until ready to use. Whip the cream and prepare the fruit. Sandwich the layers of meringue with the cream and fruit sweetened with ordinary or vanilla sugar.
Serves 6–8.

To prepare vanilla sugar:
Cut a vanilla pod in half and stand in a jar of castor or icing sugar, leave for some days before using the sugar then fill up the jar.

Vanilla Cream

½ oz. (⅛ cup) cornflour
¼ pint (⅔ cup) milk
1 oz. butter

1–2 oz. (⅛ –¼ cup) sugar
few drops vanilla essence
¼ pint (⅔ cup) thick cream

Blend the cornflour with the milk. Put into a pan with the butter and stir as it thickens; add the sugar and the essence. Cool, stirring frequently, then blend with the whipped cream.

94

Three-Fruit Meringue Pie

Fleur pastry, see page 99, or
  short crust pastry, see page 102
  made with 6 oz. (1½ cup) flour
2 lemons
1 orange
½ grapefruit

water
2½ tablespoons cornflour
4–8 oz. (½–1 cup) castor sugar,
  see method
½–1 oz. butter
2 eggs

Make the pastry and bake blind, see page 103. Grate the top
rind from the lemons, orange and grapefruit. Squeeze out the
juice, measure and add water to give ½ pint (1⅓ cups). Blend
the cornflour with the fruit juice and water, put into a pan
with the grated rind, 2–4 oz. (¼–½ cup) sugar, depending on
whether you like a sharp or sweet flavour, and the butter.
Stir over a gentle heat until thickened. Remove from the heat,
separate the eggs, add the beaten yolks. Return to the heat and
cook gently for several minutes. Taste, add even more sugar
if wished. Spoon into the pastry case.
Whisk the egg whites until very stiff, add 2 to 4 oz. (¼–½ cup)
sugar as the recipe for making meringue. Spoon over the
lemon mixture, so meringue touches the pastry rim. To serve
freshly cooked use the smaller quantity of sugar if desired.
Brown for 20 minutes in the centre of a very moderate oven,
325–350°F, Mark 3–4, or 5–8 minutes in a hot oven,
425 450°F, Mark 7–8.
To serve cold use full proportions of sugar as given in the
meringue recipe, and bake for at least 1 hour in the centre of
a very slow to slow oven, 225–250°F, Mark ½–1.

Variation:
Use all lemon juice or all orange juice and adjust the sugar in
the filling to give a pleasantly refreshing flavour.

To prepare in advance:
If preparing this dessert, or the Lime Meringue Pie, with the
biscuit crumb crust, on page 107, use the higher percentage of
sugar and longer baking time. This makes certain the
meringue will stay crisp with standing.

Savarin (French Rum Gâteau)

generous $\frac{1}{4}$ oz. yeast
1 teaspoon sugar
12 tablespoons (1 cup) tepid milk
6 oz. ($1\frac{1}{2}$ cups) plain flour
3 oz. ($\frac{3}{8}$ cup) butter
3 eggs

Syrup:
nearly $\frac{1}{2}$ pint ($1\frac{1}{4}$ cups) water
4 oz. ($\frac{1}{2}$ cup) sugar
juice 1–2 lemons
2–3 tablespoons rum
Filling:
fresh fruit

Cream the yeast with the sugar, add the milk and a sprinkling of flour. Put into a warm place for 15–20 minutes until the surface is covered with bubbles. Add the sieved flour, melted butter and beaten eggs. Mix thoroughly. Pour into a well greased and warmed 7–8-inch cake tin, or a 9–10-inch ring tin which should be 3–4 inches deep. Cover lightly and allow to prove for about 40–45 minutes, until the dough begins to rise. Bake in the centre of a hot oven, 425–450°F, Mark 6–7. Allow a total cooking time of 35–40 minutes for the cake, but 25–30 minutes for the ring tin. Reduce the heat to very moderate, 375–400°F, Mark 7–8 after 15 minutes. Meanwhile heat the water, sugar and lemon juice until a syrup-like consistency is obtained. Add the rum. Turn the cake out on to a wire cooling tray, with a plate underneath. Prick with a fine skewer and pour the hot syrup over carefully. When cool, lift on to the serving dish. Fill the centre of the ring, or cover the top of the cake with fresh fruit, i.e. oranges, apples, pears, bananas, grapes, peaches, cherries. The sides can also be decorated.
Serves 6–8.

Variation:
To make a smaller size, i.e. an 8–9-inch shallow ring, or 6–7-inch cake, use only $\frac{1}{4}$ oz. yeast, 1 teaspoon sugar, $\frac{1}{4}$ pint ($\frac{2}{3}$ cup) milk, 4 oz. (1 cup) flour, 2 oz. ($\frac{1}{4}$ cup) butter and 2 eggs. Use just over half the amount of rum syrup.

PASTRY DESSERTS

All pastry has the advantage that it may be prepared and stored in the refrigerator or home freezer before or after cooking. Choose short, sweet short or fleur pastry for sweet flans and pies. Choose puff, flaky or rough puff for vanilla slices, etc.

To make Puff Pastry

Use equal quantities of flour and butter or a mixture of butter and fat, i.e. 8 oz. flour and 8 oz. butter (2 cups flour and 1 cup butter). Sieve the flour with a pinch salt, add water or water and a little lemon juice to mix. Roll out into an oblong. Place the neat block of butter or alternative in the centre of the dough, bring up the bottom and top parts of the dough to cover the butter and form a neat shape. Turn at right angles, seal the ends; depress the dough at regular intervals and roll briskly and lightly. Repeat the process of folding into 3, turning, etc. 7 times, putting the pastry in a cool place from time to time. Then use.

Note: A recipe that says 8 oz. puff pastry means pastry made with 8 oz. (2 cups) flour, etc. You will need to buy 1 lb. frozen puff pastry as an alternative.

To make Rough Puff Pastry

Use three-quarters fat to the flour; use all butter or all margarine, or a mixture of butter or margarine and fat, i.e. 8 oz. flour and 6 oz. butter, etc. (2 cups flour and $\frac{3}{4}$ cup butter). Cut the butter or alternative fat into small pieces, drop into the flour sieved with the salt. Mix with water, or water and lemon juice, then roll, fold, etc. as puff pastry above but allow 5 rollings.

To make Flaky Pastry

Use the same proportions of fat as rough puff pastry,
see opposite. Sieve the flour and salt into a basin, rub
in $\frac{1}{3}$ of the butter, or alternative fat, then bind with water or
water and a little lemon juice. Roll out to an oblong shape.
Divide the remaining fat into equal portions. Cover two-thirds
of the dough with small pieces of fat. Fold as puff pastry,
turn, seal the edges etc. Roll out again and repeat with the
remaining fat. Give a total of 3 rollings.

Fleur Pastry

3 oz. ($\frac{3}{8}$ cup) butter or best
   quality margarine
2 oz. ($\frac{1}{4}$ cup) castor sugar

1 egg yolk
6 oz. ($1\frac{1}{2}$ cups) flour, preferably
   plain
little cold water

Cream the butter or margarine and sugar until soft and light.
Beat in the egg yolk, add the sieved flour, blend with a
palette knife. Gradually stir in enough water to bind.

Vanilla Slices (Milles Feuilles)

puff pastry made with 8 oz.
  (2 cups) flour, etc.
Filling:
$\frac{1}{2}$ pint ($1\frac{1}{3}$ cups) thick cream
sugar to taste

few drops vanilla essence
jam or jelly
little sieved icing sugar, optional

Roll the pastry out until wafer thin. Cut into about 15 or 18
fingers. Put on to baking trays or sheets, leave in a cool place
for about 30 minutes; this makes sure they keep a good shape.
Bake just above the centre of a very hot oven, 475°F, Mark
8–9. Bake for approximately 10 minutes at this high
temperature until well risen and golden, then lower the heat
to very moderate, 325–350°F, Mark 3–4, or switch the oven
off for about 5 minutes. Allow to cool then trim the edges with
a very sharp knife.
Whip the cream, add a little sugar and vanilla essence. Spread
one-third of the slices with the cream, top with another slice,
then with the jam or jelly and a final pastry slice. Dust with
sieved icing sugar.
Makes 5 or 6.
Note: Flaky or rough puff are not as good in this recipe as
puff pastry.

Variations:
Three layers of pastry give a tall and very impressive slice,
but two layers of pastry are often used, in which case spread
the bottom layer of pastry with jam or jelly and then with
cream, and top with the second layer of pastry.
Coat the top of the slices with glacé icing.

Economy hint:
Fill the slices with vanilla cream (page 94) instead of whipped
cream.

To prepare in advance:
Make and bake the pastry and store in an airtight tin away
from cakes. Reheat gently if the pastry has lost its crispness,
cool then fill.

Short Crust Pastry

8 oz. (2 cups) flour, preferably plain
pinch salt

4 oz. ($\frac{1}{2}$ cup) fat*
cold water to mix

*This can be cooking fat, margarine, butter or a mixture of these fats. All cooking fat gives a very crisp crumbly pastry and you may like to use $3\frac{1}{2}$ oz. (just under $\frac{1}{2}$ cup) only.

Sieve the flour and salt. Cut the fat into convenient-sized pieces and drop into the bowl. Rub in with the tips of your fingers until the mixture looks like fine breadcrumbs. Do not overhandle. Lift the flour and fat as you rub them together so you incorporate as much air as possible and keep the mixture cool. Gradually add water to give enough moisture to bind the ingredients together. Use a palette knife to blend. Flour varies a great deal in the amount of liquid it absorbs, but you should require about 2 tablespoons water. When blended, form into a neat ball of dough with your fingers. Put on to a lightly floured pastry board, and roll out to a neat oblong or round about $\frac{1}{4}$ inch in thickness unless the recipe states to the contrary. Always roll in one direction and do not turn the rolling pin, instead lift and turn the pastry. This makes sure it is not stretched badly.
Cook as the individual recipes. Generally short crust pastry needs a hot oven, 425–450°F, Mark 7–8, to set the pastry, but you may need to reduce the heat after a time.

Variations:
Sweet short crust pastry: Add up to 1 oz. ($\frac{1}{8}$ cup) sugar to the flour and salt.
Nut pastry: Add up to 2 tablespoons finely chopped nuts to the flour, etc. This is delicious with fruit pies.

To prepare in advance:
Either store the uncooked pastry in wrapped foil or polythene in the refrigerator or freezer or bake the pastry shell and store in an airtight tin.

Strawberry Cream Pie

Fleur pastry, page 99
1½ lb. (scant 5 cups) firm
  strawberries
generous ¼ pint (good ⅔ cup)
  thick cream

2–4 oz. (¼–½ cup) sugar
¼ pint (⅔ cup) water
1½ level teaspoons arrowroot or
  cornflour

Roll out the pastry and line an 8-inch flan ring, which has
been set on an up-turned baking tin, or a flan dish. Fill with
greased greaseproof paper, crusts of bread or beans, or with
foil. Bake empty, this is called baking 'blind', for about
15 minutes until set, in the centre of a moderately hot oven,
375–400°F, Mark 5–6, then remove paper, bread, beans or
foil. Continue baking the flan case until golden brown, then
cool.
Slice about half the strawberries neatly and mash the rest. Mix
the mashed strawberries with most of the whipped cream and
some of the sugar and put into the pastry case. Blend the rest
of the sugar – the amount depends upon personal taste, the
water and arrowroot or cornflour. Put into a saucepan, stir
over a low heat until thick and clear. Add the sliced
strawberries, heat for 1 minute only, then allow mixture to
become cold. Spoon over the cream mixture and decorate with
the last of the cream.
Serves 5–6.

Lime Meringue Pie

biscuit crumb crust, page 107
2 limes*
water
$2\frac{1}{2}$ tablespoons cornflour

4–8 oz. ($\frac{1}{2}$–1 cup) castor sugar,
  see method
$\frac{1}{2}$–1 oz. butter
2 eggs
Decoration:
1 lime slice

*Use bottled or fresh lime juice. Allow 4–5 tablespoons bottled juice and add grated lemon rind, if fresh limes are not available.

Prepare the biscuit crumb crust, see page 107. Grate the top rind from the limes, squeeze out juice, measure and add water to give $\frac{1}{2}$ pint ($1\frac{1}{3}$ cups). Blend the cornflour with the lime juice and water, put into a pan with the grated rind, 2–4 oz. ($\frac{1}{4}$–$\frac{1}{2}$ cup) sugar, depending on whether you like a sharp or sweet flavour, and the butter. Stir over a gentle heat until thickened. Remove from the heat, separate the eggs, and add the beaten yolks. Return to the heat and cook gently for several minutes. Taste, and add even more sugar if wished. Spoon onto the biscuit crumb case.
Whisk the egg whites until very stiff, add 2 or 4 oz. ($\frac{1}{4}$–$\frac{1}{2}$ cup) sugar. Spoon over the lime mixture, so the meringue touches the pastry rim. Set the meringue as outlined in the recipe on page 95.

FRUIT PIES AND TARTS

The term 'pie' is generally used to denote a deep-dish pie, with a topping of pastry. A 'plate-tart' or 'plate-pie' means pastry underneath as well as above.

When the recipe states '6 oz. pastry' it means pastry made with 6 oz. (1½ cups) flour, etc., not the total weight of pastry.

Cheese and Cherry Turnovers:

Make 8 oz. (2 cups) short crust pastry, or use one of the variations. Roll out and cut into 4 squares. Put 1 oz. (⅛ cup) cream cheese and a few stoned ripe cherries in the centre of each square. Damp the edges of the pastry, fold to make a triangle. Seal the edges with a fork. Brush with a little egg white or water and a light dusting of sugar. Bake for approximately 20–25 minutes in the centre of a hot oven, 425–450°F, Mark 7–8, reducing the heat after about 15 minutes to very moderate, 325–350°F, Mark 3–4.
Serves 4.

Spiced Pumpkin Pie:

Make, but do not bake, a pastry shell as the recipe on page 103. Cook and mash 1 lb. pumpkin. Blend this with 2 oz. (good ½ cup) brown sugar, ½ teaspoon ground ginger, ½ teaspoon ground cinnamon, ½ teaspoon mixed spice, 2 eggs and ¼ pint (⅔ cup) thin cream or milk. Spoon into the pastry case. Bake for 10 minutes in the centre of a hot oven, 425–450°F, Mark 7–8, then lower the heat to very moderate for a further 30 minutes, until pastry and filling are brown.
Serves 4–6.

Apple and Raisin Pie:

Peel and slice 1½ lb. apples, put into a pie dish with a very little water, 3 oz. (¾ cup) raisins, sugar or golden syrup to

106

taste. Make 6 oz. (1½ cups) short crust pastry, or use the variations. Roll out the pastry to a size to cover the dish, plus a little extra. Damp the edges of the pie dish, make strips of pastry to fit this, damp these then top with the rest of the pastry. Neaten the edges and bake as for pumpkin pie. **Serves 4–6.**

A plate pie may be made the same way but use about 9 oz. (2¼ cups) pastry and omit the water.

Biscuit Crumb Crust

8 oz. (4 cups) cream crackers   2 oz. (¼ cup) castor sugar
4 oz. (½ cup) butter

Crush the biscuits. Cream the butter and sugar, and add the biscuit crumbs. Form into a flan case. When using this mixture for flans such as the Strawberry Cream Pie, see page 103, simply chill to set, or crisp for a few minutes only in the oven. It is quite satisfactory if baked with a meringue topping as recipe on page 104.

Rich Cheesecake

7½–8 oz. (4 scant cups) semi-sweet biscuits

4 oz. (½ cup) butter

6 oz. (¾ cup) castor sugar

1½ lb. (3 cups) cream or cottage cheese

2 eggs

flavouring, see below

Crush the biscuits between two sheets of paper. Put into a basin and blend with the melted butter. Line the base and sides of a 7–8-inch oven-proof serving dish (about 2–3 inches deep), or cake tin with a loose base, with the crumb mixture and allow to set for about 1 hour in a cool place.

Cream the cheese with the sugar and eggs. If using cottage cheese, which gives a lighter texture than cream cheese, this may be sieved. Add flavourings: this can be the grated rind of 1–2 lemons plus about 1 tablespoon lemon juice or ½–1 teaspoon vanilla essence, or a little mixed spice; or you can put some firm fresh fruit, strawberries, diced pineapple or halved apricots over the crumb mixture.

Spread the cheese mixture over the crumbs and bake in the centre of a slow oven, 300°F, Mark 2, for 30–40 minutes until set. Turn off the heat, but keep the cheesecake in the oven until cold, this prevents it wrinkling. It is a good idea to chill this overnight if possible before removing from the tin.

If liked, decorate with fresh fruit as in the picture, or with cream.

Serves 8–10.

Variations:

Sultana and Spice Cheese Cake: Omit the lemon rind and juice, blend in the spice and 2–3 oz. (up to ⅔ cup) sultanas plus 1 tablespoon cornflour.

Sultana Rum Cheese Cake: Soak 2–3 oz. (up to ⅔ cup) sultanas in 2½ tablespoons rum, blend with the cheese together with 1 oz. (¼ cup) cornflour.

Economy hint:

Use finely grated pieces of Cheddar cheese, it does not matter if these are very stale, blended with 4 tablespoons top of the milk or thin cream.

Choosing Savouries

Many people enjoy a savoury at the end of a meal, in addition to, or instead of a dessert. The easiest savoury is to have a very attractive cheese tray with a well chosen selection of cheese, biscuits or fresh bread, butter, salad and fresh fruit.

When choosing a cheese tray:
Have a well balanced variety of cheeses –
a) Hard, familiar cheeses, for the conservative palate, such as Cheddar, Cheshire, etc.
b) Cheese with a real 'bite', i.e. Stilton, Danish Blue, or Roquefort.
c) A mild creamy cheese or cheese spread.
d) A low calorie cottage cheese.
e) One of the soft, but highly flavoured cheeses, such as Camembert or Brie.
f) A less usual cheese, such as a smoked cheese, or Raisin de Tôme.

Toasted Savouries:
These are generally popular and very simple to prepare. Put fried mushrooms on toast; sardines on toast; or make the following:

Angels on Horseback:
Season oysters and flavour with a squeeze of lemon juice. Remove the rinds from rashers of streaky bacon, halve and wrap the bacon round the oysters. Secure with wooden cocktail sticks and grill or bake until the bacon is crisp. Serve on fingers of hot buttered toast.

110

Cold Cheese Soufflé

3 eggs
aspic jelly to set $\frac{3}{4}$ pint (2 cups)
$\frac{1}{2}$ pint ($1\frac{1}{3}$ cups) water
$\frac{1}{4}$ pint ($\frac{2}{3}$ cup) thick cream
$\frac{1}{4}$ pint ($\frac{2}{3}$ cup) thin cream, or use
    all thick cream

4 oz. (1 cup) very finely grated
    Cheddar or Gruyère cheese
seasoning
Garnish:
gherkins
radishes
tomatoes

Separate the eggs and put the yolks into a basin. Soften and then dissolve the aspic jelly in the very hot water. Whisk on to the egg yolks and continue whisking until blended. Allow to cool and to begin to stiffen slightly.

Meanwhile whisk the thick cream until it holds a shape, then gradually whisk in the thin cream, cheese and seasoning. Fold into the aspic jelly mixture. Lastly fold in the stiffly whisked egg whites. Spoon into a prepared soufflé dish, see page 88, and allow to set. Remove the band of paper and garnish with pieces of gherkin, radish, if liked and tomato.

Serves 6–8.

Note: The amount of aspic gives a very lightly set soufflé which is ideal, but it must be given adequate time to set. If worried about the time then use enough aspic to set 1 pint ($2\frac{2}{3}$ cups).

To prepare in advance:

This refers to recipes on page 110 also. Put the cheeses on the tray with twists of orange, radishes, small bunches of grapes and cover with polythene, so the cheeses do not dry out. Toasted snacks cannot be kept waiting for a long period, but I find that the unbuttered toast can be kept in a cool oven, 275–300°F, Mark 1–2, the topping prepared also, covered and kept warm. This simply means buttering the hot toast and putting the topping over.

The soufflé above is better if not kept longer than 24 hours. If made too soon it becomes over-firm.

Choosing Wines

Never let price be your only consideration when buying wines. There are some excellent inexpensive wines.

It is wise to sample an unfamiliar wine before offering it at a party; buy $\frac{1}{2}$ a bottle beforehand and try it out. Individual bottles may vary slightly, but this should give you a good idea of the quality of the particular wine. When buying the large amount check it is the same year as the sample you tried. Allow about $\frac{1}{2}$ bottle of wine per person.

Serve white wines and rosé wines well chilled. Do not over-chill though, otherwise they lose their flavour.

Serve red wines at room temperature, and try and draw the corks about an hour before serving if possible.

The suggestion of serving a white wine with fish, poultry and mild flavoured dishes is simply that the flavour is more delicate and blends better with these kinds of food, just as the more full-flavoured and robust red wines blend with beef, game and dishes that are strong in taste. A rosé wine is a good 'mixer' with most foods.

The following are just some of the most familiar wines.

Red Wines:
Nuits St. George; Beaune; Beaujolais; Pommard; Mouton-Rothchild; Médoc St. Emilion; Volnay; Valpolicello (Italian).

White Wines:
Pouilly-Fuissé; Graves; Meursault; Puligny-Montrachet; Riesling (German); Soave di Verona (Italian).

Rosé Wines:
Tavel rosé; Graves rosé; Mateus rosé (Portuguese).

Wine Drinks

The following wine cup is an example of the way in which inexpensive wine can be used to make an interesting drink. It is ideal for buffet parties.

Cider, alcoholic or non-alcoholic for children, could be used in place of the white wine; omit the brandy and add ginger ale for additional flavour.

Wine Cup

2 lemons
1–2 oranges
$\frac{1}{2}$ pint ($1\frac{1}{3}$ cups) water
2–3 oz. ($\frac{1}{4}$–$\frac{3}{8}$ cup) sugar
ice cubes
2 bottles white wine

miniature bottle or wineglass
  brandy
Decoration:
cucumber slices
orange slices
sprigs borage or mint, optional

Pare the rind from the lemons and oranges very thinly. Squeeze out the juice and put on one side. Simmer the peel in the water for about 5 minutes. Add the sugar and stir until dissolved. Strain and allow to cool, then blend with the fruit juices.

Put the ice into a serving bowl, add the fruit mixture, wine and brandy. Stir gently to mix, then decorate with the cucumber, orange slices and herbs, when these are available. All recipes based on this make about 16 glasses, unless stated otherwise.

Variations:
Use only $\frac{1}{4}$ pint ($\frac{2}{3}$ cup) water with the fruit rinds.
Use weak, well strained China tea in place of water.
Use a rosé wine and Maraschino instead of white wine and brandy, top with sliced peaches and cherries.
Use only $\frac{1}{4}$ pint ($\frac{2}{3}$ cup) water, then add $\frac{1}{2}$ pint ($1\frac{1}{3}$ cups) soda water just before serving.

Parties

The dishes in the early part of the book will enable you to choose menus for dinner or luncheon parties.
In the pages that follow are suggestions for special parties.

Serve either a mixture of drinks, or just white and red wines – the latter is much easier for the host and hostess – or serve champagne for a special occasion. The non-vintage champagnes are excellent.
The recipes on pages 7, 18 and 19 are all suitable for cocktail savouries.
In addition have dishes of olives, or gherkins, or cocktail onions, or potato crisps, or nuts, etc., or serve a few dishes of each.
Cut small dice of cheese or make tiny balls of cream cheese, dice ham or roll slices of ham into tiny rolls, dice melon or make it into balls, drain canned pineapple cubes. Put these foods, together with prawns, gherkins, rolls of salami or any other interesting foods on to cocktail sticks and press the cocktail sticks into grapefruit or red cabbage.
Allow about 6 small savouries per person.
When planning to serve mixed drinks then allow:
Sherry – 12–15 glasses per bottle.
Wines – $\frac{1}{2}$ bottle per person.
Spirits – a bottle gives 16 doubles or 32 singles.
In addition you will need soda water, tonic water, dry ginger.
Beers and cider – a minimum of 1 pint.
Always have soft drinks and tomato juice available.

BUFFET PARTIES

When serving a buffet party menu choose the dishes that blend well, and that are both easy to serve and eat. It is

115

difficult to deal with large slices of meat, for example, if you are given just a fork.

Many of the dishes in this book are very suitable for a buffet. This is a menu I would suggest for a combination of hot and cold dishes.

Hors d'oeuvre	Avocado tartlets, see page 18
and/or	Melon Balls with lemon sauce, see page 10
Soup	Crab Bisque, see page 23
Fish	Fish vol-au-vents, see page 38
Poultry or	Creamed Turkey Duchesse, see page 55, or
Meat	Chicken Pilau, see page 48, or serve a selection of cold meats as on page 66, cutting these into small elegant pieces.
Desserts	Crème Brûlée, see page 80
	Lemon Soufflé, see page 88
	Celebration Cake, see below, if it is a special occasion

Cheese Board and fresh fruit

Celebration Cake

Cake:
1½ lb. (3 cups) margarine or butter
1½ lb. (3 cups) castor sugar
grated rind or 3 oranges
grated rind of 2 lemons
12 eggs
1½ lb. (6 cups) self-raising flour,
   or plain flour and 6 level
   teaspoons baking powder
4 tablespoons orange juice

Filling:
1½ lb. (3 cups) butter
2 lb. (6 cups) sieved icing sugar
little grated lemon and orange rind
2 tablespoons lemon or orange
   juice
yellow colouring

Icing:
1½ lb. (4½ cups) sieved icing sugar
3 tablespoons lemon juice
little water

The three cake tiers are 11-inch, 9-inch and 7-inch. The amount of mixture given above is sufficient for all three tiers. Choose shallow cake tins, rather than sandwich tins.

Cream the margarine or butter with the sugar until soft and light. Add the finely grated rind of the oranges and lemons – be careful that you do not use any of the bitter white pith. Gradually beat in the eggs. If the mixture shows signs of

116

curdling add a little of the sieved flour. Fold in the sieved self-raising flour, or plain flour and baking powder. Next add the orange juice.

Grease and flour the cake tins or line with greased greaseproof paper. Put the mixture into the tins, as you will see the cakes are not much deeper than a Victoria sandwich. Bake just above the centre of a very moderate oven, 325–350°F, Mark 3–4. The 7-inch layer takes about 30 minutes. The 9-inch layer about 35–40 minutes and the 11-inch layer about 40–45 minutes. Lower the heat for the large cake if it is becoming too brown. Turn the cakes out of the tins carefully and allow to cool.

Make up the butter icing for both the filling and the decoration. Cream the butter and sieved icing sugar, add a little grated lemon and orange rind and the fruit juice. Tint golden with a few drops of yellow food colouring. Split each cake and sandwich together with some of the butter icing. Spread the base of the 9-inch cake with some butter icing and put on to the 11-inch cake. Spread the base of the 7-inch cake with some of the butter icing and put on to the 9-inch cake. Make up lemon flavoured glacé icing to coat the whole cake. This must be very soft so it flows over the cakes easily. Blend the sieved icing sugar with the lemon juice and enough water to give a flowing consistency. Pour over the cakes and allow to set. Lift carefully on to the serving tray and decorate with a piping of butter icing, and bows of ribbon.

This gives about 40 portions.

TEA AND COFFEE PARTIES

If you invite friends to afternoon tea or to morning or evening coffee most of the preparations can be done well beforehand.

For a special tea menu:
Small sandwiches, see below
Fruit bread or muffins, see opposite
One special cake, such as those from pages 91–97,
and a choice of Indian or China tea.

To serve with coffee:
If mid-morning then most people would enjoy a hot muffin or biscuits.
For evening coffee then offer small savouries, see pages 7, 18 and 19, and/or sandwiches and some kind of gâteau.

Some Interesting Sandwiches

Ribbon Sandwiches:
Make sandwiches with one slice of white and one slice of brown bread, then cut into narrow strips.

Pinwheel Sandwiches:
Spread thin slices of buttered fresh bread with the filling, remove crusts, roll like a Swiss roll, then cut into thin fingers.

Open Sandwiches:
Put the topping over just one slice of buttered bread; choose a variety of breads for the base.

Sandwich fillings should not be too substantial. Try:
Scrambled egg blended with finely chopped smoked salmon, or green pepper or ham or chicken; cream or cottage cheese blended with sliced banana, dipped in lemon juice, or chopped pineapple, or chopped nuts; pâté with cucumber and lettuce.

118

Spiced Date Bread

1 lb. (2 cups) stoned dates
12 tablespoons (1 cup) milk
2 oz. ($\frac{1}{4}$ cup) margarine
12 oz. (3 cups) self-raising flour
pinch salt

$1\frac{1}{2}$ level teaspoons baking powder*
2 level teaspoons mixed spice
2 oz. ($\frac{1}{4}$ cup) sugar
1 egg

*Or plain flour and $4\frac{1}{2}$ teaspoons baking powder.

Put the dates, milk and margarine into a saucepan. Heat
gently until the margarine has melted. Sieve the flour, salt,
baking powder and spice together. Add these, and the sugar
and the egg to the date mixture in the saucepan.
Beat well, then spoon into a well greased 2–3 lb. loaf tin.
Bake for 45 minutes in the centre of a moderate oven,
350–375°F, Mark 4–5, then lower the heat to very moderate,
325–350°F, Mark 3–4, and cook for a further 10–15 minutes,
or until firm to the touch. Turn out carefully.

Variations:
Coffee Date Bread: Use either all weak coffee, or half coffee
and half milk.
Date and Nut Bread: Add a small quantity of chopped nuts.

Nut Muffins

8 oz. (2 cups) self-raising flour*
pinch salt
2 oz. ($\frac{1}{4}$ cup) sugar
3 oz. ($\frac{3}{4}$ cup) chopped nuts

2 eggs
2 oz. ($\frac{1}{4}$ cup) butter, melted
$\frac{1}{4}$ pint ($\frac{2}{3}$ cup) milk

*Or plain flour sieved with 2 teaspoons baking powder.

Sieve the flour and salt, add the rest of the ingredients and
beat until a smooth mixture. Grease and warm deep patty
tins. Spoon in the mixture and bake just above the centre of a
moderate to hot oven 375–400°F, Mark 5–6, for about 12
minutes until firm. Serve fresh with butter.
Makes about 12.

Mocha Hazel-Nut Gâteau

6 oz. ($\frac{3}{4}$ cup) butter or margarine
6 oz. ($\frac{3}{4}$ cup) castor sugar
3 large eggs
5 oz. ($1\frac{1}{4}$ cup) self-raising flour,
  with plain flour use $1\frac{1}{4}$ level
  teaspoons baking powder
$\frac{1}{2}$ oz. cocoa
$1\frac{1}{2}$ oz. (nearly $\frac{1}{2}$ cup) very finely
  chopped hazel-nuts
1 tablespoon strong coffee

Filling:
10–12 oz. ($1\frac{1}{4}$–$1\frac{1}{2}$ cup) butter or
  margarine
1–$1\frac{1}{4}$ lb. (3–$3\frac{3}{4}$ cups) sieved
  icing sugar
1–$1\frac{1}{2}$ tablespoons coffee essence
  or very strong coffee
3–4 tablespoons chopped
  hazel-nuts
whole hazel-nuts to decorate

Cream the butter or margarine and sugar, and gradually add the beaten eggs. Then fold in the sieved self-raising flour or plain flour and baking powder and cocoa. Add the chopped hazel-nuts and coffee. Divide the mixture between two 8–8$\frac{1}{2}$-inch greased and floured sandwich tins and bake for 20–25 minutes above the centre of a moderate oven, 350–375°F, Mark 4–5, until firm to the touch. Turn out carefully and allow to cool.

Make the butter icing by creaming the butter or margarine with the sieved icing sugar and coffee, the variation in amounts depends on the thickness and firmness preferred. Use about $\frac{1}{4}$ of the mixture to sandwich the cakes together and another $\frac{1}{4}$ to coat the sides. Roll the cake in the chopped nuts, then cover the top of the cake with some of the remaining icing. Pipe rosettes on top with the last of the icing. Decorate with whole hazel-nuts.

Gives 8–10 slices.

To prepare in advance:
Although the cake keeps reasonably well for several days it will keep even better if it is iced, then stored in an airtight tin, or frozen and wrapped in polythene.

Economy hint:
Hazel-nuts are expensive so use chopped walnuts instead in both the cake and the icing.

PICNICS
AND BARBECUES

Eating out of doors is enjoyable for most members of the family, but especially for the younger generation. A picnic menu can be simple or ambitious – if travelling by car you can take a wide variety of dishes.

For a simple picnic menu:
Sandwiches of various kinds, wrapped in polythene or foil so they do not dry.
Lettuce, in polythene; tomatoes, if you are sure they will not become squashed.
Cheese and fresh fruit or
Cheese and Cherry Turnovers, see page 106.
Hot or cold drinks in flasks.

For a more ambitious picnic menu:
In Winter: Soup in a warmed vacuum flask.
In Summer: Chilled soup or iced fruit juices or chilled melon, see page 10, in a wide necked vacuum flask.
Main dish: Ham en croûte, page 64, either hot or cold. If wrapped in foil immediately it comes from the oven, it will remain hot for some time, or modern insulated picnic bags keep food hot or cold. Another good picnic dish is a curry, see pages 51–52, either hot or cold, with crisp rolls. The stews or casserole dishes in this book may be put into heated wide necked vacuum flasks and served as a hot main course.
Food continues to cook in the flask, so do not over-cook.
Salads: Pack in polythene bags or boxes, foil or screwtopped jars. Take dressings separately, so the salad does not become too soft.
Desserts: Pies, such as 3-Fruit Meringue Pie, page 95, should be carried in their baking dishes, or have vacuum flasks of fruit salad and ice cream, or take fresh fruit and cheese.
Remember crushed ice to chill the drinks.

Barbecue Fare

All kinds of tender meat, some fish and poultry can be cooked directly over the barbecue. If you wish to cook less tender meat, then choose a good stew recipe and simmer in a pan.
It is traditional that fairly highly spiced sauces are served with the food or the food is basted with a well-flavoured mixture during cooking.
Do not start cooking too early over the barbecue, time the cooking so the food is eaten as soon as it is cooked.
Tender steaks, chops or cutlets, joints of chicken, as well as whole joints, can be barbecued. If the fire is really hot the cooking time will be virtually the same as when cooking at home, but turn the joints, etc. frequently so they are evenly browned.
The recipe on page 124 is a good basting sauce for most meats. The variations give suggestions for adapting this sauce for the more delicately flavoured fish and chicken.

Kebabs

These always look interesting and have the advantage of cooking quickly.
Choose lean tender meat such as beef, pork, veal, lamb, ham or chicken, and small sausages and rolls of bacon. Put the meat on long metal skewers with various vegetables or fruits. Brush with melted butter or oil, or the sauce on page 124, and cook until tender, basting well during cooking.
Never eat the food from the metal skewers directly it is cooked for the skewers become very hot; remove with a fork.

Devilled Sauce

3 large onions
$\frac{1}{4}$ pint ($\frac{2}{3}$ cup) olive or frying oil*
1–2 tablespoons Worcestershire
    sauce
up to 1 teaspoon Tabasco or chilli
    sauce

shake cayenne pepper
pinch curry powder
good pinch salt
$\frac{1}{4}$ pint ($\frac{2}{3}$ cup) red wine
$\frac{1}{4}$ pint ($\frac{2}{3}$ cup) beef stock

*Enough to baste a joint or 6 large steaks, etc.

Chop or grate the onions very finely, then mix with the oil and Worcestershire and Tabasco or chilli sauce. Add the pepper, curry powder and salt. Brush the meat with this mixture just before cooking, then baste with the mixture during cooking. Add the wine and stock towards the end of the cooking time and heat to make a sauce.
Serves 6.

Variations:
To thicken the sauce: Either blend 2 tablespoons tomato ketchup with the wine and stock, this thickens slightly as well as giving extra flavour, or blend 1 tablespoon cornflour with the wine and stock, and heat until thickened; then add the onion mixture.
To serve with fish: Use 1 onion only and add the grated rind and juice of 1–2 lemons to the oil. Use all white wine, or half white wine and half water or fish stock. The sauce can be thickened with tomato ketchup, as suggested in the variation above, or with cornflour.
To serve with poultry: Add 1–2 cloves crushed garlic to the onions – these can be used with meat also.
Be rather more sparing with the sauces and add finely chopped fresh thyme towards the end of the cooking period.

ENTERTAINING CHILDREN

The kind of food provided must vary according to the age of the children and the time of day. Modern older children often have very adult tastes and even small children seem to prefer a good selection of savoury dishes, rather than all sweet foods. There are certain foods that are popular with most children:

Sausages:
Served on sticks – hot or cold. These can be made more sophisticated for older children if arranged round a bowl of a savoury, but not too hot, dip, see page 126.
Sandwiches: With fairly familiar fillings or toppings, i.e. cheese, eggs, sardines, ham, honey. Small rolls, split and buttered and topped with the ingredients, are quick to prepare and look more interesting than ordinary sandwiches.
Yeast-type buns:
I find older children love fresh buns, and yeast cookery is most economical, see recipe below.
Interesting biscuits (cookies):
You could buy biscuits and top them with a simple icing to make them more original.
Ice cream:
The home-made variety is a pleasant change.

Pinwheel Buns

Yeast mixture:
1 lb. (4 cups) plain flour,
   preferably strong bread type
pinch salt
generous $\frac{1}{2}$ oz. yeast
1 teaspoon sugar
$\frac{1}{2}$ pint ($1\frac{1}{3}$ cups) tepid water
   or milk

Filling:
2 oz. ($\frac{1}{4}$ cup) margarine
2 oz. ($\frac{1}{4}$ cup) sugar
3 oz. ($\frac{3}{4}$ cup) sultanas
Icing:
6–8 oz. (up to $1\frac{1}{2}$ cups) sieved
   icing sugar
little water or lemon juice

Sieve the flour and salt into a bowl. Cream the yeast and sugar, add most of the tepid liquid, which should be blood heat. Make a well in the centre of the flour, pour in the yeast liquid, sprinkle flour over the top. Leave in a warm place until the surface is covered with bubbles.

Knead well to make an elastic dough, adding more liquid if needed. You can tell if the mixture is sufficiently kneaded, if the mark of a floured finger comes out readily. Cover the dough with a cloth or polythene and allow to double its size – this will take about $1\frac{1}{2}$ hours at room temperature but will vary according to the weather.

Knead again and roll out very thinly to make a smooth oblong. Spread with the softened margarine, the sugar and sultanas. Roll, like a Swiss roll, then cut into about 15 slices. Put these, cut side uppermost, on warmed greased baking trays. Allow the dough to rise for 15 minutes, and then bake for about 10–12 minutes just above the centre of a hot to very hot oven, 450–475°F, Mark 7–8. Check the buns are not browning too quickly after 5–6 minutes and reduce the heat if necessary. Cool, and then spread with icing made by blending the sugar and water or lemon juice.

Makes about 15.

Tomato Dip

$\frac{1}{2}$ pint ($1\frac{1}{3}$ cups) tomato ketchup   3 tablespoons mayonnaise
2 teaspoons made mustard

Blend together the three ingredients. Taste and adjust mixture according to personal taste. If too sweet add a little more mayonnaise; if too hot add a little cream.
Serve in a bowl with the sausages around.
Serves 6–8.

Index

Figures in italics refer to illustrations

Alaska flan 79
American salad 76, 77
Apple and raisin pie 106
Apple sauce 62
Apple water ice 83
Argentine beef stew with beans and
   corn 44, 45
Artichokes vinaigrette 12, 13
Asparagus parmesan 12
Asparagus polonaise 12
Asparagus vinaigrette 12
Aspic mould 66
Aubergine:
   Beef ratatouille 43
   Lamb ratatouille 43
   Pork ratatouille 43
   Ratatoulle 74
Avocado and bacon rolls 18
Avocado cream dip 14
Avocado tartlets 18
Avocado hors d'oeuvre 6

Barbecues 123
Beans:
   To serve beans 70
   Locro de Trigo 44, 45
Béchamel sauce 39
Beef:
   Argentine beef stew with beans
      and corn (Locro de trigo) 44, 45
   Beef en croûte 64
   Beef ratatouille 43
   Hungarian paprika stew (Goulash) 47
   Ragout of beef and prunes 41, 42
   Sweet curry 51, 53
Bigarade sauce 63
Biscuit crumb crust 107
Borscht, creamed 27
Bread sauce 58
Breads *see* Tea breads
Broccoli, to serve 70
Buffet parties 115–16

Canapés 7
Carving poultry 59
Cauliflower, to serve 70
Celebration cake 116–17
Celery à la King 71
Cheese tray 110
Cheese biscuits 7
Cheese and cherry turnovers 106
Cheese pastry 19
Cheese spreads for canapés 7
Cheese straws 19
Cheesecake 108, 109
Cold Cheese soufflé 111
Chestnut stuffing 63
Chicken:
   Chaudfroid of chicken 66
   Chicken Chambertin 27
   Chicken chowder 26, 28
   Chicken pilau 48, 49
   Chicken vol-au-vents 66
   Creamed chicken duchesse 55
   Creamed chicken soup 26
   Hungarian paprika chicken 50
   Oriental chicken 54

Roast chicken 58
   Terrine of chicken 20, 21
Chocolate orange sauce 87
Chocolate sauce 87
Chocolate sauce, economical 87
Choux pastry 72
Chowders 26–28
Clam chowder 26
Coffee date bread 119
Coffee parties 118–20
Coffee walnut layer cake 92, 93
Consommé 22
Coupe Jacques 86
Courgette hors d'oeuvre 6
Courgettes à la provençale 68, 75
Crab bisque 23
Cranberry sauce 59
Cream:
   To make a lighter cream 90
   To whip fresh cream 90
   Cream desserts 79–81
   Cream flan 79
   Vanilla cream 94
Creamed borscht 27
Creamed chicken soup 26
Creamed kidney soup 24, 25
Creamed turkey duchesse 55
Crème brulée 80, 81
Crème Chambertin 27, 29
Croûtons 71
Curry, sweet 51, 53
Date:
   Coffee date bread 119
   Date and nut bread 119
   Spiced date bread 119
Dips:
   Avocado cream dip 14
   Kipper and grapefruit dip 15
   Melon and pineapple dip 15
Duchesse potatoes 70
Duck:
   Casserole of duck 60, 61
   Duck in honey and chestnut sauce 60
   Roast duck 62
Fennel mayonnaise 34
Fish:
   To choose fish dishes 30
   To poach fish 30
   Chaudfroid of fish 31
   Chaudfroid mould of fish 31
   Cold fish dishes 30, 31
   Fish vol-au-vents 37, 38
   Fritto misto (Italian fried fish) 35, 36
   Kebabs of fish 30
   Mixed fish cocktail 6
   Scalloped fish 35
Flaky pastry 99
Flan case, to make 79
Fleur pastry 99
French dressing 76
French pork pâté 5, 11
French rum gâteau (Savarin) 96, 97
Fritto misto (Italian fried fish) 35, 36
Frosted melon cocktail 8
Frosted tomato cocktail 8, 9
Frosting 92
Fruit salad, fresh 78

Fruit Melba 86
Fruit pies and tarts 106
Fruits for ice cream 82

Goose:
   To carve goose 59
   Roast goose 62
Goulash or gulyas 47
Green mayonnaise 34

Haddock soufflé 39
Ham chowder 26
Ham en croûte 64, 65
Hare:
   Casserole of hare 56
   Hare in Madeira sauce 56, 57
Hungarian paprika chicken 50
Hungarian paprika stew 47

Ice cream and iced desserts:
   Alaska flan 79
   Apple water ice 83
   Basic cream ice 82
   Coupe Jacques 86
   Flavourings 82
   Fruit Melba 86
   Pacific delight 84, 85
   Poires Hélène 86
   Sundaes 86
Italian fried fish (Fritto misto) 35, 36

Kebabs 123
Kebabs of fish 30
Kidney:
   Creamed kidney soup 24, 25
Kipper and grapefruit dip 15

Lamb:
   Lamb en croûte 64
   Lamb pilau 48
   Lamb ratatoulle 43
   Tajine tfaia (Moroccan lamb dish) 46
Lemon:
   Lemon soufflé 88, 89
   Melon balls with lemon sauce 1, 10
   Orange and lemon syllabub 90
   Syllabub 90
Lime meringue pie 104, 105
Lobster chowder 26
Locro de Trigo 44, 45

Mayonnaise:
   Basic recipe 34
   Fennel mayonnaise 34
   Green mayonnaise 34
   Mayonnaise in a liquidizer 34
Meat dishes. *See also* Beef, Lamb etc.
   To choose meat dishes 40
   Cold meat dishes 66
   Kebabs 123
Melba sauce 86
Melon:
   Economical melon hors d'oeuvre 6
   Frosted melon cocktail 8
   Melon balls with lemon sauce 1, 10
   Melon and pineapple dip 15
Meringue gâteau 94

Milles feuilles 100, *101*
Mocha hazelnut gâteau 120
Mocha sauce 87
Moroccan lamb dish (Tajine tfaia) 46

Nut muffins 119
Nut pastry 102

Onion à la King 71
Onions florentine 71
Open sandwiches 118
Orange:
   Chocolate orange sauce 87
   Orange (Bigarade) sauce 63
   Orange layer cake 91
   Orange and lemon syllabub 90
   Orange soufflé 88
   Sweeter orange sauce 63
Oriental chicken 54
Pacific delight 84, *85*
Paprikascsirke 50
Parsley and thyme stuffing 59
Pastry. *See also* Pies, Tarts
   Cheese pastry 19
   Choux pastry 72
   Flaky pastry 99
   Fleur pastry 99
   Nut pastry 102
   Puff pastry 98
   Rough puff pastry 98
   Shortcrust pastry 102
   Sweet shortcrust pastry 102
Pâté:
   Pâté de grillotin (French pork
      pâté) 5, 11
   Smoked salmon pâté 16
   Taramasalata 16, *17*
   Toppings for canapés 7
Pear:
   Poires Hélène 86
Peas, to serve 70
Pheasant:
   Creamed pheasant duchesse 55
Picnics 122
Pies:
   Apple and raisin pie 106
   Cheese and cherry turnovers 106
   Lime meringue pie 104, *105*
   Spiced pumpkin pie 106
   Strawberry cream pie 103
   Three-fruit meringue pie 95
Pineapple:
   Melon and pineapple dip 15
   Pacific delight 84, *85*
Pinwheel sandwiches 118
Platter anglaise 66
Poires Hélène 86
Pork:
   Hungarian paprika pork 50
   Pâté de grillotin (French pork
      pâté) 5, 11
   Pork ratatouille 43
Potato:
   Creamed turkey duchesse 55
   Duchesse potatoes 70
   Potatoes dauphine 72, *73*
   Scalloped potatoes 70

Poultry. *See also* Chicken, Duck etc.
   To carve poultry 59
   To serve roast poultry 59
Prune:
   Casserole of duck 60
   Ragoût of beef and prunes *41*, 42
Puff pastry 98
Pumpkin pie, spiced 106

Ragoût of beef and prunes *41*, 42
Ratatouille 68, *69*, 74
Ratatouille as hors d'oeuvre 6
Ribbon sandwiches 118
Rice:
   Chicken pilau 48, *49*
   Lamb pilau 48
Rough puff pastry 98

Sage and onion stuffing 62
Salads:
   To choose salads 76
   American salad 76, *77*
   Fresh fruit salad 78
Salmon:
   To eke out smoked salmon 6
Salmon soufflé 39
   Smoked salmon topping for
      canapés 7
   Smoked salmon pâté 16
Sandwiches:
   Fillings for sandwiches 118
   Open sandwiches 118
   Pinwheel sandwiches 118
   Ribbon sandwiches 118
Sauces:
   Apple sauce 62
   Béchamel sauce 39
   Bread sauce 58
   Chocolate orange sauce 87
   Chocolate sauce 87
   Cranberry sauce 59
   Lemon sauce 10
   Melba sauce 86
   Mocha sauce 87
   Orange (Bigarade) sauce 63
   Orange sauce (sweeter) 63
Savouries 110–11
Savarin 96, *97*
Scalloped fish 35
Scalloped potatoes 70
Shellfish. *See also* Crab, Lobster etc.
   Mixed fish cocktail 6
   Toppings for canapés 7
Sherry, amounts to allow 115
Shortcrust pastry 102
Smoked salmon *see* Salmon
Soufflés:
   To prepare a soufflé dish 88
   Cold cheese soufflé 111
   Haddock soufflé 39
   Lemon soufflé 88, *89*
   Orange soufflé 88
   Salmon soufflé 39
   Tuna soufflé 39
Soups:
   Chicken Chambertin 27
   Chicken chowder 26, *28*

Clam chowder 26
Consommé 22
Crab bisque 23
Creamed borscht 27
Creamed chicken soup 26
Creamed kidney soup 24, *25*
Crème Chambertin 27, *29*
Ham chowder 26
Lobster chowder 26
Spiced date bread 119
Spiced pumpkin pie 106
Strawberry cream pie 103
Stuffing:
   Chestnut stuffing 63
   Parsley and thyme stuffing 59
   Sage and onion stuffing 62
Sultana rum cheesecake 108
Sultana and spice cheesecake 108
Sundaes 86
Sweet curry 51, *53*
Sweet shortcrust pastry 102
Syllabub 90
Tajine tfaia 46
Taramasalata 16, *17*
Tarts:
   Avocado tartlets 18
   Cream flan 79
   Fruit pies and tarts 106
Tea and coffee parties 118–20
Tea breads:
   Coffee date bread 119
   Date and nut bread 119
   Spiced date bread 119
Terrine of chicken 20, *21*
Three-fruit meringue pie 95
Toasted savouries 110
Tomato cocktail, frosted 8, *9*
Trout Nansen 32, *33*
Tuna soufflé 39
Turkey:
   To carve turkey 59
   Creamed turkey duchesse 55
   Roast turkey 58

Vanilla cream 94
Vanilla slices (Milles feuilles) 100, *101*
Vanilla sugar 94
Veal:
   Hungarian paprika stew 47
   Hungarian paprika veal 50
Vegetables. *See also* artichoke etc.
   To keep vegetables hot 68
   Fresh vegetables as hors d'oeuvre 6
Vienna pudding 80
Vol-au-vent:
   Chicken vol-au-vent 66
   Fish vol-au-vents *37*, 38
   Vol-au-vent cases 38

Wines 112
Wine cup *113*, 114